GROWING in Jesus

Handbook

Becoming More Like Jesus
by Studying His Life

Mark and Ernestine Finley

Pacific Press®
Publishing Association
Nampa, Idaho | www.pacificpress.com

Cover design by Gerald Monks
Cover design resources from Goodsalt | Phil McKay
Inside design by Aaron Troia

The authors assume full responsibility for the accuracy of all facts and quotations as cited in this book.

Purchase additional copies of this book by calling toll-free 1-800-765-6955 or by visiting AdventistBookCenter.com.

Library of Congress Cataloging-in-Publication Data

Names: Finley, Mark, 1945- author. | Finley, Ernestine, author.
Title: Growing in Jesus : handbook / Mark and Ernestine Finley.
Description: Nampa, Idaho : Pacific Press Publishing Association, 2021. |
    Summary: "A study guide for growing in your personal relationship with
    Jesus"— Provided by publisher.
Identifiers: LCCN 2021001132 | ISBN 9780816367382 (paperback) | ISBN
    9780816367399 (ebook)
Subjects: LCSH: Jesus Christ—Person and offices—Biblical teaching—Text-
    books.
Classification: LCC BT207 .F565 2021 Suppl. |
    DDC 232—dc23
LC record available at https://lccn.loc.gov/2021001132

January 2021

Contents

Preface

The *Growing in Jesus Handbook* is specially designed as an easy-to-use study guide on the life of Christ. Biblical insights are combined with statements from the inspired pen of Ellen White to develop an inspiring picture of the life, teachings, and ministry of Jesus in the light of the great controversy between good and evil.

Each Bible study shares the hopeful picture of Jesus triumphing over the principalities and powers of hell. In addition to presenting the uplifting story of Jesus' miracles, parables, and lifestyle teachings, this handbook covers the major doctrines of the Bible in the context of Jesus' own teaching. Topics such as salvation in Christ alone, loving obedience to His commandments, the beauty of the Sabbath, the glory of His soon return, and the joy of the resurrection and eternity are unfolded in the setting of His own words.

The *Growing in Jesus Handbook* can be used in a variety of ways. Many pastors and laypeople will use it to give Bible studies to their friends and neighbors. It is designed to supplement such traditional Bible studies as Search for Certainty or Discover, which are easily available. It can also be used as a Bible-marking series for midweek meetings in harmony with the *Growing in Jesus* lesson books. Public evangelists may find it helpful to use as a follow-up to their evangelistic meetings. Small groups meeting in the home will also appreciate its content.

Jesus said, "And I, if I be lifted up from the earth, will draw all men unto me" (John 12:32, KJV). It is our prayer that as you study these pages yourself and share these insights with others, you will be drawn closer to the Savior and experience the joy of a daily, intimate relationship with the One who loves you more than you can ever imagine.

Mark and Ernestine Finley

Jesus, the Eternal, Everlasting God

Revelation 1:8, 11	Jesus is "the Alpha and the Omega, the Beginning and the End."
Hebrews 1:1–4	Jesus is the Creator.
Colossians 1:16	Jesus created all things.
Isaiah 9:6	Jesus is everlasting.
Hebrews 1:8	The Father declares Jesus to be God.
John 8:58	Jesus declares Himself to be God.
Luke 2:9–14	The angels declare Jesus to be God.
Matthew 1:21–23	The prophets declare Jesus to be God.
John 20:28	The disciples declare Jesus to be God.
John 10:33	The Jews declare Jesus to be God.
Matthew 27:54	The Roman centurion declares Jesus to be God.
Mark 5:2–7	The demons declare Jesus to be God.
Micah 5:2	Jesus' actions are everlasting.
John 17:5	Jesus existed with the Father before the world was created.
Hebrews 1:10–12	The Father establishes the eternal nature of Christ.
Matthew 1:23	Jesus is Immanuel, "God with us."
John 14:9	From the days of eternity, Jesus was one with the Father.
Colossians 1:15–17	Jesus is "the firstborn over all creation."
Psalm 89:20, 27	David, eighth son of Jesse, is called the firstborn.
John 8:58	Jesus said, "Before Abraham was, I AM."
Micah 5:2	Jesus is the self-existent One from the days of eternity.

Isaiah 9:6	Jesus is the "Mighty God, Everlasting Father, Prince of Peace."
Revelation 1:8	Jesus is the One who is, was, and is to come.
John 14:9	"He who has seen [Jesus] has seen the Father."
2 Corinthians 4:6	The glory of God is seen in the face of Jesus Christ.
John 1:1–3, 14	"In the beginning was the Word, . . . and the Word was God."
John 17:3	Eternal life is to know Jesus Christ.
John 15:9, 13	Jesus, God's only begotten Son, is love.
John 15:15	Jesus calls us friends.
John 17:3	Jesus' greatest desire is that they may know "the only true God."

FOR FURTHER STUDY

Jesus' divinity revealed

"In the Teacher sent from God, heaven gave to men its best and greatest. He who had stood in the councils of the Most High, who had dwelt in the innermost sanctuary of the Eternal, was the One chosen to reveal in person to humanity the knowledge of God" (*Education*, 73).

Jesus existed from eternity

"The Lord Jesus Christ, the divine Son of God, existed from eternity, a distinct person, yet one with the Father" (*Selected Messages*, book 1, 247).

"The Son of God shared the Father's throne, and the glory of the eternal, self-existent One encircled both" (*Patriarchs and Prophets*, 36).

"There were some who looked with favor upon Lucifer's insinuations

6

against the government of God. Although they had heretofore been in perfect harmony with the order which God had established, they were now discontented and unhappy because they could not penetrate His unsearchable counsels; they were dissatisfied with His purpose in exalting Christ. These stood ready to second Lucifer's demand for equal authority with the Son of God. But angels who were loyal and true maintained the wisdom and justice of the divine decree and endeavored to reconcile this disaffected being to the will of God. Christ was the Son of God; He had been one with Him before the angels were called into existence. He had ever stood at the right hand of the Father" (*Patriarchs and Prophets*, 38).

"In speaking of his pre-existence, Christ carries the mind back through dateless ages. He assures us that there never was a time when He was not in close fellowship with the eternal God. He . . . had been with God as one brought up with Him" (*Evangelism*, 615).

"From the days of eternity the Lord Jesus Christ was one with the Father; He was the 'image of God,' the image of His greatness and majesty, 'the outshining of His glory.' It was to manifest this glory that He came to our world. To this sin-darkened earth He came to reveal the light of God's love,—to be 'God with us.' Therefore it was prophesied of Him, 'His name shall be called Immanuel' " (*The Desire of Ages*, 19).

"Since Jesus came to dwell with us, we know that God is acquainted with our trials, and sympathizes with our griefs. Every son and daughter of Adam may understand that our Creator is the friend of sinners. For in every doctrine of grace, every promise of joy, every deed of love, every divine attraction presented in the Saviour's life on earth, we see 'God with us' " (*The Desire of Ages*, 24).

"The name of God, given to Moses to express the idea of the eternal presence, had been claimed as His own by this Galilean Rabbi. He had announced Himself to be the self-existent One. He who had been promised to Israel, 'whose goings forth have been from of old, from the days of eternity.' Micah 5:2" (*The Desire of Ages*, 469, 470).

Jesus, the eternal, self-existent, uncreated One

"Jehovah, the eternal, self-existent, uncreated One, Himself the Source and Sustainer of all, is alone entitled to supreme reverence and worship" (*Patriarchs and Prophets*, 305).

"Jehovah is the name given to Christ. . . . 'Trust ye in the Lord forever; for in the Lord Jehovah is everlasting strength' " (*Signs of the Times*, May 3, 1899, 2).

Jesus—one with the Eternal Father in nature, character, and purpose

"Christ, the Word, the only begotten of God, was one with the eternal Father—one in nature, in character, in purpose" (*Patriarchs and Prophets*, 34).

"From all eternity, Christ was united with the Father, and when He took upon Himself human nature, He was still one with God" (*Signs of the Times*, Aug. 2, 1905, 10).

Jesus the Word was God

"While God's Word speaks of the humanity of Christ when upon this earth, it also speaks decidedly regarding His pre-existence. The Word existed as a divine being, even as the eternal Son of God, in union and oneness with His Father. From everlasting He was the Mediator of the covenant, the one in whom all nations of the earth, both Jews and Gentiles, if they accepted Him, were to be blessed. 'The Word was with God, and the Word was God.' Before men or angels were created, the Word was with God, and was God" (*Evangelism*, 615, 616).

Jesus the Eternal One is worthy of our worship

"Jehovah, the eternal, self-existent, uncreated One, Himself the

Source and Sustainer of all, is alone entitled to supreme reverence and worship. Man is forbidden to give to any other object the first place in his affections or his service. Whatever we cherish that tends to lessen our love for God or to interfere with the service due Him, of that do we make a god" (*Patriarchs and Prophets*, 305).

"The world was made by Him, 'and without Him was not anything made that was made.' (John 1:3). If Christ made all things, He existed before all things. The words spoken in regard to this are so decisive that no one need be left in doubt. Christ was God essentially, and in the highest sense. He was with God from all eternity, God over all, blessed forevermore.

"The Lord Jesus Christ, the divine Son of God, existed from eternity, a distinct person, yet one with the Father. He was the surpassing glory of heaven" (*Selected Messages*, book 1, 247).

Jesus Christ, the divine Son of God, is the eternal, self-existent, uncreated One who existed from all eternity. Therefore, He is worthy of our worship.

2

Jesus and the Great Controversy

1 John 4:7–11, 16	God's character is love.
Jeremiah 31:3	God loves you "with an everlasting love."
Philippians 2:5–8	Jesus reveals His love for the human race.
John 3:16	God's love is revealed in Christ's sacrifice of love.
John 8:44	Satan's character is one of lies and selfishness.
Romans 6:23	Satan's way is death. "The gift of God is eternal life."
Hebrews 2:14	In His death, Christ has destroyed the power of the devil.
Psalm 62:11	God is more powerful than all the forces of evil.
Psalm 104:5	Jesus is the Creator of all things.
Revelation 4:11	Jesus alone is worthy of our worship.
Ezekiel 28:12–15	Lucifer was created perfect then chose to rebel against God.
1 John 3:8	Sin originated in the devil.
Isaiah 14:12–14	Lucifer desired to rule rather than serve.
Psalm 145:17	"The Lord is righteous in all His ways."
Revelation 12:7, 8	"War broke out in heaven" because of Satan's rebellion.
Revelation 12:9	The devil was cast out of heaven.
Exodus 34:6	The Lord is merciful, gracious, long-suffering.
1 John 4:16	God's love is the sign that distinguishes His followers.
Hebrews 4:14–16	Jesus is our High Priest who welcomes us into God's presence.
Hebrews 6:17–20	Jesus has entered the heavenly sanctuary for us.
Ezekiel 28:19	Satan will cease to exist forever.

Revelation 22:3, 4	The great controversy ends in victory for Christ.
Philippians 2:9, 10	Jesus is exalted by the Father and worshiped by all heaven.
Revelation 5:8–10	All of heaven praises Jesus because He is worthy to receive glory, honor, and power because He redeemed us.

FOR FURTHER STUDY

Jesus' true character

"It was Satan that prompted the world's rejection of Christ. The prince of evil exerted all his power and cunning to destroy Jesus; for he saw that the Saviour's mercy and love, His compassion and pitying tenderness, were representing to the world the character of God" (*The Great Controversy*, 501).

"God desires from all His creatures the service of love—service that springs from an appreciation of His character. He takes no pleasure in a forced obedience; and to all He grants freedom of will, that they may render Him voluntary service" (*Patriarchs and Prophets*, 34).

"In the contest between Christ and Satan, during the Saviour's earthly ministry, the character of the great deceiver was unmasked. Nothing could so effectually have uprooted Satan from the affections of the heavenly angels and the whole loyal universe as did his cruel warfare upon the world's Redeemer" (*The Great Controversy*, 501).

The Father's struggle

"Said the angel, 'Think ye that the Father yielded up His dearly beloved Son without a struggle? No, no. It was even a struggle with the God of heaven, whether to let guilty man perish, or to give His beloved Son to die for him.' Angels were so interested for man's salvation that there

11

could be found among them those who would yield their glory and give their life for perishing man, 'But,' said my accompanying angel, 'that would avail nothing. The transgression was so great that an angel's life would not pay the debt. Nothing but the death and intercessions of His Son would pay the debt and save lost man from hopeless sorrow and misery' " (*The Story of Redemption*, 45).

The cross and the Father's pain

"The cross is a revelation to our dull senses of the pain that, from its very inception, sin has brought to the heart of God" (*Education*, 263).

"It was not merely to accomplish the redemption of man that Christ came to the earth to suffer and to die. He came to 'magnify the law' and to 'make it honorable.' Not alone that the inhabitants of this world might regard the law as it should be regarded; but it was to demonstrate to all the worlds of the universe that God's law is unchangeable. . . . The death of Christ proves it immutable" (*The Great Controversy*, 503).

"If the law could be changed, man might have been saved without the sacrifice of Christ; but the fact that it was necessary for Christ to give His life for the fallen race, proves that the law of God will not release the sinner from its claims upon him. It is demonstrated that the wages of sin is death" (*Patriarchs and Prophets*, 70).

Christ's supremacy

"The exaltation of the Son of God as equal with the Father was represented as an injustice to Lucifer, who, it was claimed, was also entitled to reverence and honor" (*Patriarchs and Prophets*, 37).

"He [Satan] had sought to falsify the word of God and had misrepresented His plan of government, claiming that God was not just in imposing laws upon the angels; that in requiring submission and obedience from His creatures, He was seeking merely the exaltation of Himself. It was therefore necessary to demonstrate before the inhabitants of heaven, and of all the worlds, that God's government is just, His law perfect. . . . The true character of the usurper and his real object must be understood by all. He must have time to manifest himself by his wicked works" (*Patriarchs and Prophets*, 42).

The origin of evil

"The entrance of sin into heaven cannot be explained. If it were explainable, it would show that there was some reason for sin. But as there was not the least excuse for it, its origin will ever remain shrouded in mystery" (*Advent Review and Sabbath Herald*, March 9, 1886).

"It is impossible to explain the origin of sin so as to give a reason for its existence. Yet enough may be understood concerning both the origin and final disposition of sin to make fully manifest the justice and benevolence of God in all His dealings with evil. Nothing is more plainly taught in Scripture than that God was in no wise responsible for the entrance of sin; that there was no arbitrary withdrawal of divine grace, no deficiency in the divine government, that gave occasion for the uprising of rebellion. Sin is an intruder, for whose presence no reason can be given. It is mysterious, unaccountable; to excuse it is to defend it. Could excuse for it be found, or cause be shown for its existence, it would cease to be sin" (*The Great Controversy*, 492, 493).

Lucifer's pride

"Not content with his position, though honored above the heavenly host, he [Lucifer] ventured to covet homage due alone to the Creator. Instead of seeking to make God supreme in the affections and allegiance of all created beings, it was his endeavor to secure their service and loyalty to himself. And coveting the glory with which the infinite Father had invested His Son, this prince of angels aspired to power that was the prerogative of Christ alone" (*Patriarchs and Prophets*, 35).

"Pride in his own glory nourished the desire for supremacy. The high honors conferred upon Lucifer were not appreciated as the gift of God and called forth no gratitude to the Creator. He gloried in his brightness and exaltation, and aspired to be equal with God" (*The Great Controversy*, 495).

"His disaffection was proved to be without cause, and he was made to see what would be the result of persisting in revolt. Lucifer was convinced that he was in the wrong. He saw that 'the Lord is righteous in all His ways, and holy in all His works' (Psalm 145:17); that the divine statutes are just, and that he ought to acknowledge them as such before all heaven. Had he done this, he might have saved himself and many angels. He had not at that time fully cast off his allegiance to God. . . . He nearly reached the decision to return, but pride forbade him. It was too great a sacrifice for one who had been so highly honored to confess that he had been in error, that his imaginings were false, and to yield to the authority which he had been working to prove unjust" (*Patriarchs and Prophets*, 39).

War in heaven

"The inhabitants of heaven and of other worlds, being unprepared to comprehend the nature or consequences of sin, could not have seen the justice and mercy of God in the destruction of Satan. Had he been immediately blotted from existence, they would have served God from fear rather than from love. The influence of the deceiver would not have been fully destroyed, nor would the spirit of rebellion have been utterly eradicated. Evil must be permitted to come to maturity. For the good of the entire universe through ceaseless ages Satan must more fully develop his principles; that his charges against the divine government might be seen in their true light by all created beings, that the justice and mercy of God and the immutability of His law might forever be placed beyond all question" (*The Great Controversy*, 498, 499).

"In great mercy, according to His divine character, God bore long with Lucifer. The spirit of discontent and disaffection had never before been known in heaven. It was a new element, strange, mysterious, unaccountable. Lucifer himself had not at first been acquainted with the real nature of his feelings; for a time he had feared to express the workings and imaginings of his mind; yet he did not dismiss them. He did not see whither he was drifting. . . . Though he had left his position as covering cherub, yet if he had been willing to return to God, acknowledging the Creator's wisdom, and satisfied to fill the place appointed him in God's great plan, he would have been reinstated in his office" (*Patriarchs and Prophets*, 39).

Jesus exalted as High Priest

"It was the work of the priest in the daily ministration to present before God the blood of the sin offering, also the incense which ascended with the prayers of Israel. So did Christ plead His blood before the Father in behalf of sinners, and present before Him also, with the precious fragrance of His own righteousness, the prayers of penitent believers. Such was the work of ministration in the first apartment of the sanctuary in heaven" (*The Great Controversy*, 420, 421).

"The intercession of Christ in man's behalf in the sanctuary above is as essential to the plan of salvation as was His death upon the cross. By His death He began that work which after His resurrection He ascended to complete in heaven. We must by faith enter within the veil, 'whither the forerunner is for us entered.' Hebrews 6:20. There the light from the cross of Calvary is reflected. There we may gain a clearer insight into the mysteries of redemption. The salvation of man is accomplished at an infinite expense to heaven; the sacrifice made is equal to the broadest demands of the broken law of God. Jesus has opened the way to the Father's throne, and through His mediation the sincere desire of all who come to Him in faith may be presented before God" (*The Great Controversy*, 489).

The great controversy ended

"The great controversy is ended. Sin and sinners are no more. The entire universe is clean. One pulse of harmony and gladness beats through the vast creation. From Him who created all, flow life and light and gladness, throughout the realms of illimitable space. From the minutest atom to the greatest world, all things, animate and inanimate, in their unshadowed beauty and perfect joy, declare that God is love" (*The Great Controversy*, 678).

Colossians 1:15	Jesus is the image of God.
Colossians 1:16	Jesus is the Creator.
Colossians 1:17	Jesus is the Sustainer of all living things.
Colossians 1:18	Jesus is the Preeminent One.
Colossians 1:19, 20	Jesus is the fullness of the Godhead.
Colossians 1:20	Jesus is the Redeemer.
Hebrews 1:1, 2	Jesus, our Creator, is the "heir of all things."
Genesis 1:26, 27	Jesus, our Creator, made us in His image.
Job 38:4, 7	The "morning stars" rejoiced when Jesus created our world.
Revelation 1:20	Revelation reveals the stars are the angels.
Ephesians 3:9	God created all things through Jesus.
Genesis 1:1	"In the beginning God created the heavens and the earth."
Psalm 33:6, 9	God made the heavens through the power of His word.
Genesis 1:27–31	Jesus created Adam and Eve on the sixth day of the Creation week.
Genesis 2:7	Jesus, the Creator, breathed the breath of life into man.
Genesis 2:1, 2	God ended His work of creation and rested the seventh day.
Genesis 2:2, 3	"God blessed the seventh day and sanctified it."
Genesis 2:4	"This is the history of the heavens and the earth."
Isaiah 45:18	God formed the earth to be inhabited.
Genesis 2:16, 17	God allowed man to eat of every tree except "the tree of knowledge of good and evil."

Genesis 2:17	God's warning to Adam and Eve regarding "the tree of knowledge of good and evil" was, If you eat of it, "you shall surely die."
Genesis 3:4	"The serpent said to the woman, 'You will not surely die.' "
Genesis 3:6	Eve ate the fruit and gave it to her husband, and he ate also.
Romans 6:23	"The wages of sin is death, but the gift of God is eternal life."
Genesis 3:15	The first promise of a Savior (Jesus) who will create enmity between Satan and Jesus' children.
Romans 5:12, 17–19	Through Adam's disobedience, death spread to all men; through Christ's obedient life, "many will be made righteous."
Hebrews 4:15	Jesus "was in all points tempted as we are, yet without sin."
Isaiah 43:1	Jesus is our Creator and Redeemer. We are twice His, by Creation and Redemption.
Revelation 21:1–4	One day, through Jesus, sin will come to an end forever. The new earth will be restored more gloriously than at the beginning.

FOR FURTHER STUDY

Creation

"As the earth came forth from the hand of its Maker, it was exceedingly beautiful. Its surface was diversified with mountains, hills, and plains, interspersed with noble rivers and lovely lakes. . . . There were no loathsome swamps or barren deserts. Graceful shrubs and delicate flowers greeted the eye at every turn. The heights were crowned with trees more majestic than any that now exist. The air, untainted by foul miasma, was clear and healthful. The entire landscape outvied in beauty the decorated grounds of the proudest palace. The angelic host viewed the scene with delight, and rejoiced at the wonderful works of God" (*Patriarchs and Prophets*, 44).

"The creative energy that called the worlds into existence is in the word of God. This word imparts power; it begets life. Every command is a promise; accepted by the will, received into the soul, it brings with it the life of the Infinite One. It transforms the nature and re-creates the soul in the image of God" (*Education*, 126).

"Just how God accomplished the work of creation He has never revealed to men; human science cannot search out the secrets of the Most High. His creative power is as incomprehensible as His existence" (*Patriarchs and Prophets*, 113).

Creation week

"Like the Sabbath, the week originated at creation, and it has been preserved and brought down to us through Bible history. God Himself measured off the first week as a sample for successive weeks to the close of time. Like every other, it consisted of seven literal days. Six days were employed in the work of creation; upon the seventh, God rested, and He then blessed this day, and set it apart as a day of rest for man. . . .

". . . The Bible recognizes no long ages in which the earth was slowly evolved from chaos. Of each successive day of creation, the sacred record declares that it consisted of the evening and the morning, like all other days that have followed" (*Patriarchs and Prophets*, 111, 112).

The weekly cycle

"It is not because of inherent power that year by year the earth produces her bounties and continues her motion around the sun. The hand of God guides the planets and keeps them in position in their orderly march through the heavens. . . .

"God is the foundation of everything. All true science is in harmony with His works; all true education leads to obedience to His government. Science opens new wonders to our view; she soars high, and explores new depths; but brings nothing from her research that conflicts with divine revelation. Ignorance may seek to support false views of God by appeals to science, but the book of nature and the written word shed light upon each other. We are thus led to adore the Creator and to have an intelligent trust in His word" (*Patriarchs and Prophets*, 115, 116).

The creation of humanity

" 'So, God created man in His own image; . . . male and female created He them.' Here is clearly set forth the origin of the human race; and the divine record is so plainly stated that there is no occasion for erroneous conclusions. God created man in His own image. Here is no mystery. There is no ground for the supposition that man evolved by slow degrees of development from the lower forms of animal or vegetable life. Such teaching lowers the great work of the Creator to the level of man's narrow, earthly conceptions. Men are so intent upon excluding God from the sovereignty of the universe that they degrade man and defraud him of the dignity of his origin. . . . The genealogy of our race . . . traces back its origin, not to a line of developing germs, mollusks, and quadrupeds, but to the great Creator. Though formed from the dust, Adam was 'the Son of God' " (*Patriarchs and Prophets*, 44).

"He [Adam] was more than twice as tall as men now living upon the earth, and was well proportioned. His features were perfect and beautiful. . . . Eve was not quite as tall as Adam. Her head reached a little above his shoulders. She, too, was noble, perfect in symmetry, and very beautiful" (*The Story of Redemption*, 21).

"Many teach that matter possesses vital power—that certain properties are imparted to matter, and it is then left to act through its own inherent energy; and that the operations of nature are conducted in harmony with fixed laws, with which God Himself cannot interfere. This is false science, and is not sustained by the word of God" (*Patriarchs and Prophets*, 114).

Adam and Eve's fall

"He [Satan] shuddered at the thought of plunging the holy, happy pair into the misery and remorse he was himself enduring. He seemed in a state of indecision: at one time firm and determined, then hesitating and wavering. His angels were seeking him, their leader, to acquaint him with their decision. They would unite with Satan in his plans, and with him bear the responsibility and share the consequences" (*The Story of Redemption*, 28, 29).

"No longer free to stir up rebellion in heaven, Satan's enmity against God found a new field in plotting the ruin of the human race. In the happiness and peace of the holy pair in Eden he beheld a vision of the bliss that to him was forever lost. Moved by envy, he determined to incite them to disobedience, and bring upon them the guilt and penalty of sin. He would change their love to distrust and their songs of praise to reproaches against their Maker. Thus he would not only plunge these innocent beings into the same misery which he was himself enduring, but would cast dishonor upon God, and cause grief in heaven" (*Patriarchs and Prophets*, 52).

"An expression of sadness came over the face of Adam. He appeared astonished and alarmed. To the words of Eve he replied that this must be the foe against whom they had been warned; and by the divine sentence she must die. In answer she urged him to eat, repeating the words of the serpent, that they should not surely die. She reasoned that this must be true, for she felt no evidence of God's displeasure, but on the contrary realized a delicious, exhilarating influence, thrilling every faculty with new life, such, she imagined, as inspired the heavenly messengers.

"Adam understood that his companion had transgressed the command of God, disregarded the only prohibition laid upon them as a test of their fidelity and love. There was a terrible struggle in his mind. He mourned that he had permitted Eve to wander from his side. But now the deed was done; he must be separated from her whose society had been his joy. How could he have it thus? Adam had enjoyed the companionship of God and of holy angels. He had looked upon the glory of the Creator. He understood the high destiny opened to the human race should they remain faithful to God. Yet all these blessings were lost sight of in the fear of losing that one gift which in his eyes outvalued every other. Love, gratitude, loyalty to the Creator—all were overborne by love to Eve. She was a part of himself, and he could not endure the thought of separation. He did not realize that the same Infinite Power who had from the dust of the earth created him, a living, beautiful form, and had in love given him a companion, could supply her place. He resolved to share her fate; if she must die, he would die with her" (*Patriarchs and Prophets*, 56).

God's promise to Adam and Eve

" 'I will put enmity between thee and the woman, and between thy seed and her seed; it shall bruise thy head, and thou shalt bruise his heel.' Genesis 3:15. This sentence, uttered in the hearing of our first parents, was to them a promise. While it foretold war between man and Satan, it declared that the power of the great adversary would finally be broken. . . . Though they must suffer from the power of their mighty foe, they could look forward to final victory" (*Patriarchs and Prophets*, 65, 66).

God's law is unchangeable

"I saw that it was impossible for God to change His law in order to save lost, perishing man; therefore He suffered His darling Son to die for man's transgressions" (*Early Writings*, 127).

"The law of God is as sacred as God Himself. . . . The harmony of creation depends upon the perfect conformity of all beings, of everything, animate and inanimate, to the law of the Creator. God has ordained laws for the government, not only of living beings, but of all the operations of nature. . . .

"Like the angels, the dwellers in Eden had been placed upon probation; their happy estate could be retained only on condition of fidelity to the Creator's law. They could obey and live, or disobey and perish" (*Patriarchs and Prophets*, 52, 53).

"The law of God can no more be transgressed with impunity now than when sentence was pronounced upon the father of mankind" (*Patriarchs and Prophets*, 61).

Jesus' great sacrifice

"The Son of God, heaven's glorious Commander, was touched with pity for the fallen race. His heart was moved with infinite compassion as the woes of the lost world rose up before Him. But divine love had conceived a plan whereby man might be redeemed. The broken law of God demanded the life of the sinner. In all the universe there was but one who could, in behalf of man, satisfy its claims. Since the divine law is as sacred as God Himself, only one equal with God could make atonement for its transgression. Only one equal with God could make atonement for its transgression. None but Christ could redeem fallen man from the curse of the law and bring him again into harmony with Heaven. Christ would take upon Himself the guilt and shame of sin—sin so offensive to a holy God that it must separate the Father and His Son. Christ would reach to the depths of misery to rescue the ruined race" (*Patriarchs and Prophets*, 63).

The angels' part in the plan of redemption

"The angels prostrated themselves at the feet of their Commander and offered to become a sacrifice for man. But an angel's life could not pay the debt; only He who created man had power to redeem him. Yet the angels were to have a part to act in the plan of redemption. . . .

"Christ assured the angels that by His death He would ransom many, and would destroy him who had the power of death. . . .

"Then joy, inexpressible joy, filled heaven. The glory and blessedness of a world redeemed, outmeasured even the anguish and sacrifice of the Prince of life" (*Patriarchs and Prophets*, 64, 65).

The future immortality of the redeemed

"Then they that have kept God's commandments shall breathe in immortal vigor beneath the tree of life; and through unending ages the inhabitants of sinless worlds shall behold, in that garden of delight, a sample of the perfect work of God's creation, untouched by the curse of sin—a sample of what the whole earth would have become, had man but fulfilled the Creator's glorious plan" (*Patriarchs and Prophets*, 62).

4

Jesus, the Redeemer

Romans 6:23	"The wages of sin is death, but the gift of God is eternal life."
Romans 5:12	Death spread to all humans through Adam's sin.
1 John 4:9, 10	God manifests His love for us in Christ.
Matthew 5:17, 18	Jesus did not come to destroy the law but to fulfill it.
Revelation 13:8	Jesus is "the Lamb slain from the foundation of the world."
1 Peter 1:18–20	Christ "was foreordained before the foundation of the world" as our Redeemer.
Philippians 2:5–8	Christ, "equal with God," became a servant and "humbled Himself" unto "death, even the death of the cross."
John 3:16	God gave evidence of His love by sending His only begotten Son into the world that we might be saved.
Hebrews 2:9	Christ tastes death for everyone.
Matthew 27:27–30	Jesus wore a crown of thorns and was mocked and crucified.
Mark 15:13–15	The crowd cried, "Crucify Him!"
Matthew 27:46	Jesus cried, "My God, My God, why have You forsaken Me?"
Hebrews 1:13, 14	Angels were sent forth to minister to Jesus.
Micah 4:8	The blessings promised to God's people will be fulfilled.
Galatians 3:13	"Christ has redeemed us from the curse of the law."
Hebrews 2:14, 15	Jesus destroys the power of death and the devil forever.

God's law is unchangeable

"I saw that it was impossible for God to change His law in order to save lost, perishing man; therefore He suffered His darling Son to die for man's transgressions" (*Early Writings*, 127).

A way of escape

"I saw the lovely Jesus and beheld an expression of sympathy and sorrow upon His countenance. Soon I saw Him approach the exceeding bright light which enshrouded the Father. Said my accompanying angel, He is in close converse with His Father. . . . Three times He was shut in by the glorious light about the Father, and the third time He came out from the Father, His person could be seen. His countenance was calm, free from all perplexity and doubt, and shone with benevolence and loveliness, such as words cannot express.

"He then made known to the angelic host that a way of escape had been made for lost man. He told them that He had been pleading with His Father, and had offered to give His life a ransom, to take the sentence of death upon Himself, that through Him man might find pardon; that through the merits of His blood, and obedience to the law of God, they could have the favor of God and be brought into the beautiful garden and eat of the fruit of the tree of life" (*The Story of Redemption*, 42, 43).

Angels offered their lives

"The angels prostrated themselves at the feet of their Commander and offered to become a sacrifice for man. But an angel's life could not pay the debt; only He who created man had power to redeem him" (*Patriarchs and Prophets*, 64, 65).

Greatest manifestation of God's love

"The Son of God, heaven's glorious Commander, was touched with pity for the fallen race. His heart was moved with infinite compassion as the woes of the lost world rose up before Him. But divine love had conceived a plan whereby man might be redeemed. . . . Since the divine law is as sacred as God Himself, only one equal with God could make atonement for its transgression. None but Christ could redeem fallen man from the curse of the law and bring him again into harmony with heaven. . . . Christ would reach to the depths of misery to rescue the ruined race" (*Patriarchs and Prophets*, 63).

The plan of salvation vindicates the character of God

"But the plan of redemption had a yet broader and deeper purpose than the salvation of man. It was not for this alone that Christ came to the earth; it was not merely that the inhabitants of this little world might regard the law of God as it should be regarded, but it was to vindicate the character of God before the universe. . . . The act of Christ dying . . . would not only make heaven accessible to men, but before all the universe it would justify God and His Son in their dealing with the rebellion of Satan. It would establish the perpetuity of the law of God and would reveal the nature and the results of sin" (*Patriarchs and Prophets*, 68, 69).

Jesus' assurance of His unchangeable law

"If the law could be changed, man might have been saved without the sacrifice of Christ; but the fact that it was necessary for Christ to give His life for the fallen race, proves that the law of God will not release the sinner from its claims upon him. It is demonstrated that the wages of sin is death. . . . The very fact that Christ bore the penalty of man's transgression is a mighty argument to all created intelligences that the law is changeless; that God is righteous, merciful, and self-denying; and that infinite justice and mercy unite in the administration of His government" (*Patriarch and Prophets*, 70).

Redemption planned in advance

"The plan for our redemption was not an afterthought, a plan formulated after the fall of Adam. It was a revelation of 'the mystery which hath been kept in silence through times eternal' Romans 16:25, R. V. . . . From the beginning, God and Christ knew of the apostasy of Satan and the fall of man through the deceptive power of the apostate. God did not ordain that sin should exist, but He foresaw its existence, and made provision to meet the terrible emergency. So great was His love for the world, that He covenanted to give His only-begotten Son, 'that whosoever believeth in Him should not perish, but have everlasting life.' John 3:16" (*The Desire of Ages*, 22).

The Father's struggle

"Said the angel, 'Think ye that the Father yielded up His dearly beloved Son without a struggle? No, no. It was even a struggle with the God of heaven, whether to let guilty man perish, or to give His beloved Son to die for him' " (*The Story of Redemption*, 45).

An unbroken tie

"By His life and His death, Christ has achieved even more than recovery from the ruin wrought through sin. It was Satan's purpose to bring about an eternal separation between God and man; but in Christ we become more closely united to God than if we had never fallen. In taking our nature, the Saviour has bound Himself to humanity by a tie that is never to be broken. Through the eternal ages He is linked with us" (*The Desire of Ages*, 25).

God is justified

"Through Christ's redeeming work the government of God stands justified. The Omnipotent One is made known as the God of love. Satan's charges are refuted, and his character unveiled.

Rebellion can never again arise. Sin can never again enter the universe. Through eternal ages all are secure from apostasy. By love's self-sacrifice, the inhabitants of earth and heaven are bound to their Creator in bonds of indissoluble union" (*The Desire of Ages*, 26).

Our only atonement

"They [Adam and Eve] were told that since the law of Jehovah is the foundation of His government in heaven as well as upon the earth, even the life of an angel could not be accepted as a sacrifice for its transgression. Not one of its precepts could be abrogated or changed to meet man in his fallen condition; but the Son of God, who had created man, could make an atonement for him. As Adam's transgression had brought wretchedness and death, so the sacrifice of Christ would bring life and immortality" (*Patriarchs and Prophets*, 66, 67).

"When the angels should witness the agony and humiliation of their Lord, they would be filled with grief and indignation and would wish to deliver Him from His murderers; but they were not to interpose in order to prevent anything which they should behold. It was a part of the plan of redemption that Christ should suffer the scorn and abuse of wicked men, and He consented to all this when He became the Redeemer of man" (*Patriarchs and Prophets*, 65).

Christ's ultimate sacrifice

"Christ was treated as we deserve, that we might be treated as He deserves. He was condemned for our sins, in which He had no share, that we might be justified by His righteousness, in which we had no share. He suffered the death which was ours, that we might receive the life which was His. 'With His stripes we are healed' " (*The Desire of Ages*, 25).

Christ's death reconciled man to God

"Christ assured the angels that by His death He would ransom many, and would destroy him who had the power of death. . . . Sin and sinners would be blotted out, nevermore to disturb the peace of heaven or earth. He bade the angelic host to be in accord with the plan that His Father had accepted, and rejoice that, through His death, fallen man could be reconciled to God" (*Patriarchs and Prophets*, 65).

Christ as conqueror

"The great contest that had been so long in progress in this world was now decided, and Christ was conqueror. His death had answered the question whether the Father and the Son had sufficient love for man to exercise self-denial and a spirit of sacrifice. . . . With one voice the loyal universe united in extolling the divine administration" (*Patriarchs and Prophets*, 70).

Steps in the plan of salvation

Psalm 51:3; **Romans 3:23**	Acknowledge you have sinned.
John 3:16, 17	Believe that "God so loved the world . . . He gave His only . . . Son."
1 John 1:9	Confess and accept His forgiveness, believing He will cleanse you.
Acts 3:19	"Repent . . . and be converted."
John 1:12	Receive Him and become a child of God.

Believe. "The heart of God yearns over His earthly children with a love stronger than death. In giving up His Son, He has poured out to us all heaven in one gift. The Saviour's life and death and intercession, the ministry of angels, the pleading of the Spirit, the Father working above and through all, the unceasing interest of heavenly beings,—all are enlisted in behalf of man's redemption.

"Oh, let us contemplate the amazing sacrifice that has been made for us!" (*Steps to Christ*, 21).

Confess. "We should not try to lessen our guilt by excusing sin. We must accept God's estimate of sin, and that is heavy indeed. Calvary alone can reveal the terrible enormity of sin. If we had to bear our own guilt, it would crush us. But the sinless One has taken our place; though undeserving, He has borne our iniquity. 'If we confess our sins,' God 'is faithful and just to forgive us our sins, and to cleanse us from all unrighteousness.' 1 John 1:9" (*Thoughts From the Mount of Blessing*, 116).

Repent. "But must the sinner wait till he has repented before he can come to Jesus? Is repentance to be made an obstacle between the sinner and the Saviour?

"The Bible does not teach that the sinner must repent before he can heed the invitation of Christ, 'Come unto Me, all ye that labor and are heavy-laden, and I will give you rest.' Matthew 11:28. It is the virtue that goes forth from Christ, that leads to genuine repentance. . . . We can no more repent without the Spirit of Christ to awaken the conscience than we can be pardoned without Christ" (*Steps to Christ*, 26).

Receive by faith. "The world's Redeemer accepts men as they are, with all their wants, imperfections, and weaknesses; and He will not only cleanse from sin and grant redemption through His blood, but will satisfy the heart-longing of all who consent to wear His yoke, to bear His burden. It is His purpose to impart peace and rest to all who come to Him for the bread of life. . . .

"Through the right exercise of the will, an entire change may be made in your life. By yielding up your will to Christ, you ally yourself with the power that is above all principalities and powers. You will have strength from above to hold you steadfast, and thus through constant surrender to God you will be enabled to live the new life, even the life of faith" (*Steps to Christ*, 46–48).

Children of God

"Because of Christ's death on the cross, we have the privilege of becoming the children of God. This is the most wonderful and exciting news in the world. His great sacrifice is incomprehensible, but by faith, I accept it.

"Through the cross we learn that the heavenly Father loves us with a love that is infinite" (*The Acts of the Apostles*, 210).

5

Jesus, the Messiah of Prophecy

Galatians 4:4	"When the fullness of the time had come, God sent . . . His Son."
Romans 5:6	"In due time Christ died for the ungodly."
Matthew 1:18	The Holy Spirit conceived Jesus in the womb of the virgin Mary.
Luke 1:30	The angel told Mary not to be afraid because she has "found favor with God."
Isaiah 7:14	Prediction: "The virgin shall conceive and bear a Son, and shall call His name Immanuel."
Matthew 1:23	Fulfillment: "The virgin shall be with child, and bear a Son, and they shall call His name Immanuel, which is translated, 'God with us.' "
Isaiah 9:6	Jesus would "be called Wonderful, Counselor, Mighty God, Everlasting Father, Prince of Peace."
Luke 2:12	A sign for the shepherds to find Jesus was, "You will find a Babe wrapped in swaddling cloths, lying in a manger."
Luke 2:17, 18	When the shepherds saw Jesus, they told everyone what they had learned about this Child.
Numbers 24:17	Prediction: "A Star shall come out of Jacob; a Scepter shall rise out of Israel."
Matthew 2:1, 2	Fulfillment: The wise men seek to find Jesus, the "King of the Jews." They "have seen His star in the East and have come to worship Him."
Matthew 2:11	The Magi give to Baby Jesus "gold, frankincense, and myrrh."

Micah 5:2	Prediction: The exact birthplace of the Messiah to be born was Bethlehem in Judah.
Luke 2:4–7	Fulfillment: Joseph went from Nazareth "to the city of David, which is called Bethlehem. . . . And she (Mary) brought forth her firstborn Son, and wrapped Him in swaddling cloths, and laid Him in a manger, because there was no room for them in the inn."
Genesis 3:15	The first prophecy of the coming of the Messiah.
Hosea 11:1	Prediction: Hosea predicts Jesus going to Egypt. "Out of Egypt I called My Son."
Matthew 2:13	Fulfillment: "Arise, take the young Child and His mother, flee to Egypt, and stay there until I bring you word, for Herod will seek the young Child to destroy Him."
Revelation 12:4	Revelation describes Herod's satanic desire: "The dragon stood before the woman who was ready to give birth, to devour her Child as soon as it was born."
Hebrew 2:14–18	It was necessary for Jesus to take on our nature to be our Redeemer. "In all things He had to be made like His brethren."
Luke 19:10	The purpose of Jesus' coming to earth: "The Son of Man has come to seek and to save that which was lost."
Luke 2:40	"The Child grew and became strong in spirit, filled with wisdom; and the grace of God was upon Him."
Hebrews 4:15	We have a High Priest who sympathizes "with our weaknesses, [and] was in all points tempted as we are."
Luke 2:46–49	Jesus was found "in the temple, sitting in the midst of the teachers, both listening to them and asking them questions." Jesus was doing His Father's will.

FOR FURTHER STUDY

The fullness of time

"The fullness of the time had come. Humanity, becoming more degraded through ages of transgression, called for the coming of the Redeemer. Satan had been working to make the gulf deep and impassable between earth and heaven. By his falsehoods he had emboldened men in sin. It was his purpose to wear out the forbearance of God, and to extinguish His love for man, so that He would abandon the world to satanic jurisdiction" (*The Desire of Ages*, 34, 35).

The timing of Jesus' birth

"Like the stars in the vast circuit of their appointed path, God's purposes know no haste and no delay. . . . So in heaven's council the hour for the coming of Christ had been determined. When the great clock of time pointed to that hour, Jesus was born in Bethlehem" (*The Desire of Ages*, 32).

Satan trembles

"At the birth of Jesus, Satan knew that One had come with a divine commission to dispute his dominion. He trembled at the angel's message attesting the authority of the newborn King. Satan well knew the position that Christ had held in heaven as the Beloved of the Father. That the Son of God should come to this earth as a man filled him with amazement and with apprehension. He could not fathom the mystery of this great sacrifice. . . . Since he had lost heaven, he was determined to find revenge by causing others to share his fall. This he would do by causing them to undervalue heavenly things, and to set the heart upon things of earth" (*The Desire of Ages*, 115, 116).

An innumerable throng of angels

"Above the hills of Bethlehem are gathered an innumerable throng of angels. They wait the signal to declare the glad news to the world. Had the leaders in Israel been true to their trust, they might have shared the joy of heralding the birth of Jesus. But now they are passed by. . . .

". . . To those who are seeking for light, and who accept it with gladness, the bright rays from the throne of God will shine" (*The Desire of Ages*, 47).

Glory to God in the highest

"The whole plain was lighted up with the bright shining of the hosts of God. Earth was hushed, and heaven stooped to listen to the song,—

'Glory to God in the highest,
And on earth peace, good will toward men.'

"Oh, that today the human family could recognize that song! The declaration then made, the note then struck, will swell to the close of time, and resound to the ends of the earth" (*The Desire of Ages*, 48).

The wise men

"The magi learned with joy that His coming was near, and that the whole world was to be filled with a knowledge of the glory of the Lord.

"The wise men had seen a mysterious light in the heavens upon that night when the glory of God flooded the hills of Bethlehem. As the light faded, a luminous star appeared, and lingered in the sky. It was not a fixed star, nor a planet, and the phenomenon excited the keenest interest. That star was a distant company of shining angels, but of this the wise men were ignorant. Yet they were impressed that the star was of special import to them" (*The Desire of Ages*, 60).

"The magi had been among the first to welcome the Redeemer. Their gift was the first that was laid at His feet. And through that gift, what privilege of ministry was theirs! The offering from the heart that loves, God delights to honor, giving it highest efficiency in service for Him. If we have given our hearts to Jesus, we also shall bring our gifts to Him. Our gold and silver, our most precious earthly possessions, our highest mental and spiritual endowments, will be freely devoted to Him who loved us, and gave Himself for us" (*The Desire of Ages*, 65).

The first promise of a Savior

"The gospel was first preached to Adam by Christ. Adam and Eve felt sincere sorrow and repentance for their guilt. They believed the precious promise of God, and were saved from utter ruin" (*Advent Review and Herald of the Sabbath*, April 29, 1875, 138).

"Heaven and earth are no wider apart today than when shepherds listened to the angels' song. . . .

"The story of Bethlehem is an exhaustless theme. In it is hidden 'the depth of the riches both of the wisdom and knowledge of God.' Romans 11:33. We marvel at the Saviour's sacrifice in exchanging the throne of heaven for the manger, and the companionship of adoring angels for the beasts of the stall. Human pride and self-sufficiency stand rebuked in His presence. Yet this was but the beginning of His wonderful condescension" (*The Desire of Ages*, 48, 49).

Jesus' human nature

"It would have been an almost infinite humiliation for the Son of God to take man's nature, even when Adam stood in his innocence in Eden. But Jesus accepted humanity when the race had been weakened by four thousand years of sin. Like every child of Adam He accepted the results of the working of the great law of heredity. What these results were is shown in the history of His earthly ancestors. He came with such a heredity to share our sorrows and temptations, and to give us the example of a sinless life" (*The Desire of Ages*, 49).

Jesus' early life and childhood

"Since He gained knowledge as we may do, His intimate acquaintance with the Scriptures shows how diligently His early years were given to the study of God's word. And spread out before Him was the great library of God's created works. He who had made all things studied the lessons which His own hand had written in earth and sea and sky. . . . From His earliest years He was possessed of one purpose; He lived to bless others" (*The Desire of Ages*, 70).

"These adversaries of Christ had no arguments with which to meet the truths He brought home to their consciences. They could only cite their customs and traditions, and these seemed weak and vapid when compared with the arguments Jesus had drawn from the word of God and the unceasing round of nature" (*The Desire of Ages*, 208).

"Young companions urged Him [Jesus] to do as they did. He was bright and cheerful; they enjoyed His presence, and welcomed His ready suggestions; but they were impatient at His scruples, and pronounced Him narrow and strait-laced. Jesus answered, It is written, 'Wherewithal shall a young man cleanse his way? by taking heed thereto according to Thy word.' 'Thy word have I hid in mine heart, that I might not sin against thee.' Psalm 119:9, 11" (*The Desire of Ages*, 89).

Temptation is not sin

"Temptation is not sin. Jesus was holy and pure; yet He was tempted in all points as we are, but with a strength and power that man will never be called upon to endure. In His successful resistance He has left us a bright example, that we should follow His steps. If we are self-confident or self-righteous we shall be left to fall under the power of temptation; but if we look to Jesus and trust in Him we call to our aid a power that has conquered the foe on the field of battle, and with every temptation He will make a way of escape" (*Testimonies for the Church*, vol. 5, 426).

Jesus' experience in the temple

"If Joseph and Mary had stayed their minds upon God by meditation and prayer, they would have realized the sacredness of their trust, and would not have lost sight of Jesus. By one day's neglect they lost the Saviour; but it cost them three days of anxious search to find Him. So with us; by idle talk, evilspeaking, or neglect of prayer, we may in one day lose the Saviour's presence, and it may take many days of sorrowful search to find Him, and regain the peace that we have lost" (*The Desire of Ages*, 83).

6

Jesus' Baptism and the Holy Spirit

John 1:19–23	John the Baptist prepared the way for Jesus.
John 1:20–23	John declared, "I am the voice of one crying in the wilderness: make straight the way of the LORD."
John 1:25	John was asked, "Why then do you baptize if you are not the Christ, nor Elijah, nor the Prophet?"
John 1:26, 27	John claimed that the One who came after him was preferred before him.
Matthew 3:1–3	John the Baptist was the forerunner of Jesus.
John 1:29, 30	John referred to Jesus as "the Lamb of God who takes away the sin of the world!"
Revelation 13:8	Jesus is "the Lamb slain from the foundation of the world."
Hebrews 9:22	"Without [the] shedding of blood there is no remission" for sin.
Luke 3:16	John the Baptist stated, "I . . . baptize with . . . water; but One mightier than I is coming, whose sandal strap I am not worthy to loose. He will baptize you with the Holy Spirit and fire."
John 6:63	Jesus said, "It is the Spirit who gives life; the flesh profits nothing. The words that I speak to you are spirit, and they are life."
Matthew 3:11	John told the Jewish teachers, "I . . . baptize you with water unto repentance, but He who is coming . . . is mightier than I."
Matthew 3:13	Jesus set an example for us when He came from Galilee to John at the Jordan to be baptized by him.

Matthew 3:14	John objected to Jesus by saying, "I need to be baptized by You, and are You coming to me?"
Matthew 3:15	Jesus answered John and said, "Permit it to be so now, for thus it is fitting for us to fulfill all righteousness."
Matthew 3:16	"When He had been baptized, Jesus came up immediately from the water, and behold, the heavens were opened to Him, and He saw the Spirit of God descending like a dove and alighting upon Him."
Matthew 3:17	Then a voice was heard from heaven, "This is My beloved Son, in whom I am well pleased."
Acts 2:38	Peter said, "Repent, and let every one of you be baptized in the name of Jesus Christ for the remission of sins; and you shall receive the gift of the Holy Spirit."
Mark 16:16	"He who believes and is baptized will be saved; but he who does not believe will be condemned."
Acts 2:41	"Then those who gladly received his word were baptized; and that day about three thousand souls were added to them."
Matthew 28:19, 20	"Go . . . and make disciples of all the nations, baptizing them in the name of the Father and of the Son and of the Holy Spirit, teaching them to observe all things that I have commanded you; and lo, I am with you always, even to the end of the age."

FOR FURTHER STUDY

John prepares the way

"John came in the spirit and power of Elijah to proclaim the first advent of Jesus. I was pointed down to the last days and saw that John represented those who should go forth in the spirit and power of Elijah to herald the day of wrath and the second advent of Jesus" (*The Story of Redemption*, 198).

"The scripture to which John referred to is that beautiful prophecy of Isaiah [40:3]: '. . . The voice of him that crieth in the wilderness, Prepare ye the way of the Lord, make straight in the desert a highway for our God' " (*The Desire of Ages*, 134, 135).

Evidence of Jesus' divinity

"John proclaimed the coming of the Messiah, and called the people to repentance. As a symbol of cleansing from sin, he baptized them in the waters of the Jordan. Thus by a significant object lesson he declared that those who claimed to be the chosen people of God were defiled by sin, and that without purification of heart and life they could have no part in the Messiah's kingdom" (*The Desire of Ages*, 104).

Jesus' baptism meant as an example

"Jesus did not receive baptism as a confession of guilt on His own account. He identified Himself with sinners, taking the steps that we are to take, and doing the work that we must do. His life of suffering and patient endurance after His baptism was also an example to us" (*The Desire of Ages*, 111).

" 'This is My beloved Son, in whom I am well pleased,' embraces humanity. God spoke to Jesus as our representative. With all our sins and weaknesses, we are not cast aside as worthless. 'He hath made us accepted in the beloved.' Ephesians 1:6. The glory that rested upon Christ is a pledge of the love of God for us. It tells us of the power of prayer,—how the human voice may reach the ear of God, and our petitions find acceptance in the courts of heaven. . . . His love has encircled man, and reached the highest heaven. The light which fell from the open portals upon the head of our Saviour will fall upon us as we pray for help to resist temptation. The voice which spoke to Jesus says to every believing soul, 'This is My beloved child, in whom I am well pleased' " (*The Desire of Ages*, 113).

Symbolism of baptism

"Here are presented two requirements made of those who accept the gospel proclamation—faith in Jesus, and baptism. The first is the inward acceptance of the salvation so graciously provided by the vicarious death of the world's Redeemer; the second is the outward token of an inward change of life" (*The Seventh-day Adventist Bible Commentary*, vol. 5, 659).

7

Jesus' Temptations and Victory

Matthew 4:1	Jesus is tempted in the wilderness.
Hebrews 2:14, 17	Jesus partakes of our nature.
Hebrews 4:15	Jesus was tempted in all points like we are and sympathizes with our weakness.
Isaiah 52:14	Jesus was exhausted in the wilderness, and His "visage," or appearance, "was marred more than any man."

Jesus' first temptation: Appetite

Matthew 4:2, 3	Satan's temptations came after Jesus fasted in the wilderness. "And when He had fasted forty days and forty nights, afterward He was hungry. Now when the tempter came to Him, he said, 'If You are the Son of God, command that these stones become bread.' "
Matthew 4:4	Jesus answered, "It is written, 'Man shall not live by bread alone, but by every word that proceeds from the mouth of God.' "
John 14:30	There was nothing in Christ that responded to Satan's temptations.
Philippians 4:13	"I can do all things through Christ who strengthens me."
John 8:29	"The Father has not left Me alone, for I always do those things that please Him."

Jesus' second temptation: Presumption

Matthew 4:5, 6	"If you are the Son of God, throw Yourself down. For it is written: 'He shall give His angels charge concerning you.' "

1 Corinthians 10:13 "No temptation has overtaken you, but God is faithful, who will not allow you to be tempted beyond what you are able."

Jesus' third temptation: Love of the world

Matthew 4:8, 9 "The devil took Him up on an exceedingly high mountain, and showed Him all the kingdoms of the world and their glory. And he said to Him, 'All these things I will give You if You will fall down and worship me.' "

Matthew 4:10 Jesus said to him, "It is written again, you shall not tempt the Lord your God."

Matthew 4:10 "Then Jesus said to him, 'Away with you, Satan! For it is written, "You shall worship the LORD your God, and Him only you shall serve." ' "

Matthew 4:4 Jesus met Satan with "It is written."

James 4:7 "Submit to God. Resist the devil and he will flee from you."

Revelation 5:12 All heaven praises our Redeemer. "Worthy is the Lamb who was slain to receive power and riches and wisdom, and strength and honor and glory and blessing!"

FOR FURTHER STUDY

Communication with humanity

"Ever since Adam's sin, the human race had been cut off from direct communion with God; the intercourse between heaven and earth had been through Christ; but now that Jesus had come 'in the likeness of sinful flesh' (Romans 8:3), the Father Himself spoke. He had before communicated with humanity *through* Christ; now He communicated with humanity *in* Christ" (*The Desire of Ages*, 116).

Jesus' experience in the wilderness

"When Jesus was led into the wilderness to be tempted, He was led by the Spirit of God. He did not invite temptation. He went to the wilderness to be alone, to contemplate His mission and work. By fasting and prayer He was to brace Himself for the bloodstained path He must travel. But Satan knew that the Saviour had gone into the wilderness, and he thought this the best time to approach Him" (*The Desire of Ages*, 114).

Jesus' first temptation

"With Christ, as with the holy pair in Eden, appetite was the ground of the first great temptation. Just where the ruin began, the work of our redemption must begin. As by the indulgence of appetite Adam fell, so by the denial of appetite Christ must overcome" (*The Desire of Ages*, 117).

"So now the tempter seeks to inspire Christ with his own sentiments. 'If Thou be the Son of God.' . . . Would God treat His own Son thus? . . . He insinuates that God never meant His Son to be in such a state as this. 'If Thou be the Son of God,' show Thy power by relieving Thyself of this pressing hunger. Command that this stone be made bread" (*The Desire of Ages*, 118, 119).

"Weak and emaciated from hunger, worn and haggard with mental agony, 'His visage was so marred more than any man, and His form more than the sons of men.' Isaiah 52:14" (*The Desire of Ages*, 118).

Lessons from the first temptation of Jesus

"Of all the lessons to be learned from our Lord's first great temptation none is more important than that bearing upon the control of the appetites and passions. In all ages, temptations appealing to the physical nature have been most effectual in corrupting and degrading mankind. Through intemperance, Satan works to destroy the mental and moral powers that God gave to man as a priceless endowment" (*The Desire of Ages*, 122).

"The controlling power of appetite will prove the ruin of thousands, when, if they had conquered on this point, they would have had moral power to gain the victory over every other temptation of Satan" (*Counsels on Diet and Foods*, 163).

"Jesus says, 'He hath nothing in Me.' His victory is an assurance that we too may come off victors in our conflicts with the enemy" (*Counsels on Diet and Foods*, 153).

Jesus' second temptation

"But again the temptation is prefaced with the insinuation of distrust, '*If* Thou be the Son of God.' Christ was tempted to answer the 'if,' but He refrained from the slightest acceptance of the doubt. He would not imperil His life in order to give evidence to Satan" (*The Desire of Ages*, 124).

"When Satan quoted the promise, 'He shall give His angels charge over Thee,' he omitted the words, 'to keep Thee in all Thy ways;' that is, in all the ways of God's choosing. Jesus refused to go outside the path of obedience. While manifesting perfect trust in His Father, He would not place Himself, unbidden, in a position that would necessitate the interposition of His Father to save Him from death. He would not force Providence to come to His rescue, and thus fail of giving man an example of trust and submission" (*The Desire of Ages*, 125).

Knowing the Scriptures

"None but those who have fortified the mind with the truths of the Bible will stand through the last great conflict" (*The Great Controversy*, 593, 594).

"Only those who have been diligent students of the Scriptures and who have received the love of the truth will be shielded from the powerful delusion that takes the world captive" (*The Great Controversy*, 625).

"Jesus was victor in the second temptation, and now Satan manifests himself in his true character. . . .

"Placing Jesus upon a high mountain, Satan caused the kingdoms of the world, in all their glory, to pass in panoramic view before Him. . . . Jesus . . . now gazed upon a scene of unsurpassed loveliness and prosperity. Then the tempter's voice was heard: 'All this power will I give Thee, and the glory of them: for that is delivered unto me; and to whomsoever I will I give it. If Thou therefore wilt worship me, all shall be Thine.'

"Christ's mission could be fulfilled only through suffering. . . . Christ might deliver Himself from the dreadful future by acknowledging the supremacy of Satan. But to do this was to yield the victory in the great controversy" (*The Desire of Ages*, 129).

Jesus' third temptation

"Jesus met Satan with the words of Scripture. 'It is written,' He said. In every temptation the weapon of His warfare was the word of God" (*The Desire of Ages*, 120).

"Since He gained knowledge as we may do, His intimate acquaintance with the Scriptures shows how diligently His early years were given to the study of God's word" (*The Desire of Ages*, 70).

"In our own strength it is impossible for us to deny the clamors of our fallen nature. . . . Christ knew that the enemy would come to every human being, to take advantage of hereditary weakness, and by his false insinuations to ensnare all whose trust is not in God. And by passing over the ground which man must travel, our Lord has prepared the way for us to overcome" (*The Desire of Ages*, 122, 123).

"Satan trembles and flees before the weakest soul who finds refuge in that mighty name" (*The Desire of Ages*, 131).

Angels offered their lives

"The angels prostrated themselves before Him. They offered their lives. Jesus said to them that He would by His death save many, that the life of an angel could not pay the debt. . . . Jesus also told them that they would have a part to act, to be with Him and at different times strengthen Him; that He would take man's fallen nature, and His strength would not be even equal with theirs; that they would be witnesses of His humiliation and great sufferings; and that as they would witness His sufferings, and the hatred of men toward Him, they would be stirred with the deepest emotion, and through their love for Him would wish to rescue and deliver Him from His murderers; but that they must not interfere to prevent anything they should behold; and that they should act a part of His resurrection; that the plan of salvation was devised, and His Father had accepted the plan" (*Early Writings*, 150, 151).

"All these heavenly beings have one object above all others, in which they are intensely interested—His church in a world of corruption. . . .

". . . They are working for Christ under His commission, to save to the uttermost all who look to Him and believe in Him. . . .

"In their service, these armies of heaven illustrate what the church of God should be. Christ is working in their behalf in the heavenly courts, sending out His messengers to all parts of the globe, to the assistance of every suffering one who looks to Him for relief, for spiritual life and knowledge" (Letter 89c, 1897).

8
Jesus' Ministry

Jesus begins His ministry and calls His disciples

Acts 10:36	The message of the New Testament church was, Jesus is "Lord of all."
Acts 10:37	The disciples preached the Word powerfully "throughout all Judea."
Acts 10:38	"God anointed Jesus of Nazareth with the Holy Spirit and with power, who went about doing good and healing all who were oppressed by the devil, for God was with Him."
John 1:41, 42	When Andrew found Jesus, Andrew immediately found his brother and "brought him to Jesus."
John 1:43	"He [Jesus] found Philip and said to him, 'Follow Me.' "
John 1:45	Philip found Nathanael and declared that they had found the one the prophets pointed to—"Jesus of Nazareth."
John 1:46	"Philip said to him, 'Come and see.' "

Jesus begins His ministry

John 2:1, 2	Jesus, His mother, and His disciples attended "a wedding in Cana of Galilee."
John 2:3	"And when they ran out of wine, the mother of Jesus said to Him, 'They have no wine.' "
John 2:4	"Jesus said to her, 'Woman, what does your concern have to do with Me? My hour has not yet come.' "

John 17:1	"My hour has not yet come" points to the hour of Christ's crucifixion. "Father, the hour has come. Glorify Your Son, that Your Son also may glorify You."
John 2:5	"His mother said to the servants, 'Whatever He says to you, do it.' "
John 2:7, 8	"Jesus said to them, 'Fill the waterpots with water.' And they filled them up to the brim. And He said to them. 'Draw some out now and take it to the master of the feast.' "

Jesus' first miracle

John 2:9	"When the master of the feast had tasted the water that was made wine and did not know where it came from (but the servants who had drawn the water knew), the master of the feast called the bridegroom."
John 2:10	"And he said to him, 'Every man at the beginning sets out the good wine, and when the guests have well drunk, then the inferior. You have kept the good wine until now!' "
John 2:11	"The beginning of signs Jesus did in Cana of Galilee and manifested His glory; and His disciples believed in Him."
Proverbs 20:1	Jesus did not create fermented wine because "wine is a mocker, strong drink is a brawler, and whoever is led astray by it is not wise." (See also Proverbs 23:29–33, Isaiah 65:8.)

Jesus meets every need

John 1:38	Notice Jesus' model of ministry. "What are you seeking? What are your needs?"
John 2	Jesus meets a social need at the wedding feast.
John 3	Jesus meets a spiritual need, resulting in Nicodemus's conversion.

John 4	Jesus meets an emotional need in His encounter with the Samaritan woman.
John 5	Jesus meets a physical need in His healing of the man at the pool of Bethesda.
Matthew 4:23	His ministry was threefold. "Jesus went about all Galilee, teaching . . . , preaching . . . , and healing."
Matthew 4:24, 25	Jesus had a healing ministry. "Then His fame went throughout all Syria; and they brought to Him all sick people who were afflicted with various diseases and torments, and those who were demon-possessed, epileptics, and paralytics; and He healed them."
Mark 1:38	Jesus had a preaching ministry. "Let us go into the next towns, that I may preach there also, because for this purpose I have come forth."

Reasons not everyone is healed

Matthew 17:20	Our unbelief. Some lack faith.
Psalm 66:18	Willful disobedience. Cherishing sin in our hearts limits God's power in our lives. (See also Psalm 78:40–42.)
2 Corinthians 12:8, 9	God may use our weakness. We live in a broken world, and God often reveals His strength in our weakness. (See also 2 Corinthians 1:3–7.)
Mark 1:35–38	God has a greater purpose. At Capernaum, although many were healed, some were not because Christ's greater purpose was to preach the gospel and save people eternally so they would never get sick again.
John 20:30, 31	The miracles of Jesus were recorded so that "believing you may have life in His name."

FOR FURTHER STUDY

Following Jesus, the Lamb of God

"Again, the face of the prophet was lighted up with glory from the Unseen, as he cried, 'Behold the Lamb of God!' The words thrilled the hearts of the disciples. They did not fully understand them" (*The Desire of Ages*, 138).

"Leaving John, they went to seek Jesus. One of the two was Andrew, the brother of Simon; the other was John the evangelist. These were Christ's first disciples. Moved by an irresistible impulse, they followed Jesus,—anxious to speak with Him, yet awed and silent, lost in the overwhelming significance of the thought, 'Is this the Messiah?' " (*The Desire of Ages*, 138).

Sharing Jesus

"Andrew sought to impart the joy that filled his heart. Going in search of his brother Simon, he cried, 'We have found the Messias.' Simon waited for no second bidding. He also had heard the preaching of John the Baptist, and he hastened to the Saviour. The eye of Christ rested upon him, reading his character and his life history. His impulsive nature, his loving, sympathetic heart, his ambition and self-confidence, the history of his fall, his repentance, his labors, and his martyr death,—the Saviour read it all" (*The Desire of Ages*, 139).

"John directed two of his disciples to Christ. Then one of these, Andrew, found his brother, and called him to the Saviour. Philip was then called, and he went in search of Nathanael. These examples should teach us the importance of personal effort, of making direct appeals to our kindred, friends, and neighbors" (*The Desire of Ages*, 141).

Sharing in Christ's work

"No sooner does one come to Christ than there is born in his heart a desire to make known to others what a precious friend he has found in Jesus; the saving and sanctifying truth cannot be shut up in his heart" (*Steps to Christ*, 78).

"God could have reached His object in saving sinners without our aid; but in order for us to develop a character like Christ's, we must share in His work. In order to enter into His joy,—the joy of seeing souls redeemed by His sacrifice,—we must participate in His labors for their redemption" (*The Desire of Ages*, 142).

Jesus' ministry begins

"Jesus did not begin His ministry by some great work before the Sanhedrin at Jerusalem. At a household gathering in a little Galilean village His power was put forth to add to the joy of a wedding feast. Thus He showed His sympathy with men, and His desire to minister to their happiness" (*The Desire of Ages*, 144).

"Jesus answered, 'Woman, what have I to do with thee? Mine hour is not yet come.'

"This answer, abrupt as it seems to us, expressed no coldness or discourtesy. The Saviour's form of address to His mother was in accordance with oriental custom. It was used toward persons to whom it was desired to show respect. Every act of Christ's earthly life was in harmony with the precept He Himself had given, 'Honor thy father and thy mother.' Exodus 20:12.

". . . For thirty years He had been to her a loving and obedient son, and His love was unchanged; but He must now go about His Father's work" (*The Desire of Ages*, 146, 147).

The meaning of "Mine hour is not yet come"

"The words, 'Mine hour is not yet come,' point to the fact that every act of Christ's life on earth was in fulfillment of the plan that had existed from the days of eternity. . . .

"In saying to Mary that His hour had not yet come, Jesus was replying to her unspoken thought, to the expectation she cherished in common with her people. She hoped that He would reveal Himself as the Messiah and take the throne of Israel. . . .

"But though Mary had not a right conception of Christ's mission, she trusted Him implicitly. To this faith Jesus responded. It was to honor Mary's trust, and to strengthen the faith of His disciples, that the first miracle was performed" (*The Desire of Ages*, 147).

The meaning of the water and the wine

"The gift of Christ to the marriage feast was a symbol. The water represented baptism into His death; the wine, the shedding of His blood for the sins of the world. . . .

"The wine which Christ provided for the feast, and that which He gave to the disciples as a symbol of His own blood, was the pure juice of the grape. . . .

". . . The unfermented wine which He provided for the wedding guests was a wholesome and refreshing drink" (*The Desire of Ages*, 148, 149).

Jesus' method

"Christ's method alone will give true success in reaching the people. The Saviour mingled with men as One who desired their good. He showed His sympathy for them, ministered to their needs, and won their confidence. Then He bade them, 'Follow Me' " (*The Ministry of Healing*, 143).

"The Saviour made each work of healing an occasion for implanting divine principles in the mind and soul. This was the purpose of His work" (*The Ministry of Healing*, 20).

The purpose of Christ's miracles

"Christ never worked a miracle except to supply a genuine necessity, and every miracle was of a character to lead the people to the tree of life, whose leaves are for the healing of the nations" (*The Desire of Ages*, 366).

Why some prayers are not answered

"I saw that the reason why God did not hear the prayers of His servants for the sick among us more fully was, that He could not be glorified in so doing while they were violating the laws of health. And I also saw that He designed the health reform and Health Institute to prepare the way for the prayer of faith to be fully answered" (*Counsels on Diet and Foods*, 25, 26).

Glorifying Jesus

"God will not work a miracle to keep those from sickness who have no care for themselves, but are continually violating the laws of health, and make no efforts to prevent disease. When we do all we can on our part to have health, then may we expect that the blessed results will follow, and we can ask God in faith to bless our efforts for the preservation of health. He will then answer our prayer, if His name can be glorified thereby" (*Counsels on Diet and Foods*, 26).

"We should ever remember that the object of the medical missionary work is to point sin-sick men and women to the Man of Calvary" (*Counsels on Diet and Foods*, 458, 459).

Jesus' threefold ministry: Teaching, preaching, and healing

"If ever the Lord has spoken by me, He speaks when I say that the workers engaged in educational lines, in ministerial lines, and in medical missionary lines must stand as a unit, all laboring under the supervision of God, one helping the other, each blessing each. . . .

"Christ, the great Medical Missionary, is our example. . . . He healed the sick and preached the gospel. In His service, healing and teaching were linked closely together. Today they are not to be separated" (*Testimonies for the Church*, vol. 9, 169–171).

9

Jesus' Worship and the Sabbath

Luke 4:16	Jesus "went into the synagogue on the Sabbath day."
Luke 4:17	Jesus participated in Sabbath worship by reading Isaiah's prophecy.
Luke 4:18, 19	The Holy Spirit anointed Jesus to preach the gospel, heal, and proclaim freedom to the oppressed.
Luke 4:20, 21	At Sabbath worship, Jesus declared that He was the fulfillment of Isaiah's Messianic prophecy.
Acts 13:42–44	Throughout the New Testament, the disciples shared Jesus' Sabbath-keeping example with both Jews and Gentiles.
Acts 16:13	The New Testament church followed Jesus' example of Sabbath keeping. The apostle Paul met with a small group of worshipers on the Sabbath in a quiet setting outside of Philippi.
Acts 17:2, 3	Paul, as his custom was, preached for three Sabbaths, proclaiming that Christ had to suffer and rise again from the dead saying, "This Jesus whom I preach to you is the Christ."
Acts 17:4	"A great multitude of the devout Greeks, and not a few of the leading women, [were persuaded and] joined Paul and Silas."
Hebrews 10:24, 25	The apostle Paul encourages all believers not to forsake the assembling of themselves together in corporate worship.

Jesus' healing ministry on the Sabbath

John 9:14   "It was a Sabbath when Jesus made the clay and opened [the blind man's] eyes." Seven of Christ's healing miracles were performed on the Sabbath. For Christ, the Sabbath was a day of healing.

Mark 3:1, 2   Jesus cared deeply for suffering people. He was willing to face misunderstanding by healing the withered hand of a poor sufferer on the Sabbath.

Mark 3:3–6   Jesus declared, "Is it lawful on the Sabbath to do good or to do evil, to save life or to kill?" He was "grieved by the hardness of their hearts" and with compassion healed the man's withered hand.

Mark 2:23–27   Jesus states an eternal truth: "The Sabbath was made for man, and not man for the Sabbath."

Matthew 12:12   For Jesus, people are more valuable than a sheep that has fallen into a ditch; "therefore it is lawful to do good on the Sabbath."

The Sabbath as a sign of Jesus as Creator

Psalm 95:6, 7   God admonishes us to worship our Maker.

Genesis 2:1–4   When Jesus gave humanity the Sabbath, He showed it would serve three specific purposes: blessing, sanctification, and rest.

Matthew 12:8   Jesus is Lord of the Sabbath. (See also Luke 6:5.)

John 1:1–3   "All things [including the Sabbath] were made through Him [Jesus]."

Genesis 1:27   God created male and female in His own image.

Ephesians 3:9   "God . . . created all things through Jesus Christ."

Revelation 4:11   "You are worthy, O Lord,
To receive glory and honor and power;
For You created all things,
And by Your will they exist and were created."

Exodus 20:8-11	The Sabbath is a symbol of Christ's creative authority.
Ezekiel 20:12	God gave the Sabbath as a sign between Him and His people that they might know that He is Lord.
Ezekiel 20:20	God tells His people to honor, or keep holy, "My sabbaths."
Revelation 14:6, 7	God's final message to humanity is to worship Him as the Creator.

Identifying the Sabbath according to Jesus

| **Luke 23:54–24:1** | These passages list three days in succession describing which day is the Sabbath: |

1. The preparation day—"That day was the preparation"—Friday
2. The Sabbath day—The day Jesus rested in the tomb—Saturday
3. The Resurrection day—"The first day of the week"—Sunday

| **Hebrews 13:8** | Jesus does not change: He "is the same yesterday, today, and forever." |
| **Isaiah 66:22, 23** | In the new heaven and new earth, we will keep the Sabbath. |

FOR FURTHER STUDY

Jesus fulfills Isaiah's prophecy

"Jesus stood before the people as a living expositor of the prophecies concerning Himself. . . . His impressive manner and the wonderful import of His words thrilled the hearers with a power they had never felt before. The tide of divine influence broke every barrier down; like Moses, they beheld the invisible. As their hearts were moved upon by the Holy Spirit, they responded with fervent amens and praises to the Lord" (*The Desire of Ages*, 237).

Jesus healed on the Sabbath

"In the healing of the withered hand, Jesus condemned the custom of the Jews, and left the fourth commandment standing as God had given it. 'It is lawful to do well on the Sabbath days,' He declared. By sweeping away the senseless restrictions of the Jews, Christ honored the Sabbath, while those who complained of Him were dishonoring God's holy day" (*The Desire of Ages*, 287).

Jesus cleared misconceptions

"The rabbis virtually represented God as giving laws which it was impossible for men to obey. They led the people to look upon God as a tyrant, and to think that the observance of the Sabbath, as He required it, made men hard-hearted and cruel. It was the work of Christ to clear away these misconceptions" (*The Desire of Ages*, 284).

Cooking on the Sabbath

"While cooking upon the Sabbath should be avoided, it is not necessary to eat cold food. In cold weather let the food prepared the day before be heated. And let the meals, though simple, be palatable and attractive. Provide something that will be regarded as a treat, something the family do not have every day" (*Counsels for the Church*, 267).

Jesus' disciples plucked grain and ate it on the Sabbath

"Christ would teach His disciples and His enemies that the service of God is first of all. The object of God's work in this world is the redemption of man; therefore that which is necessary to be done on the Sabbath in the accomplishment of this work is in accord with the Sabbath law" (*The Desire of Ages*, 285).

Jesus cared for the sick and the suffering on Sabbath

"Divine mercy has directed that the sick and suffering should be cared for; the labor required to make them comfortable is a work of necessity, and no violation of the Sabbath. But all unnecessary work should be avoided" (*Counsels for the Church*, 267).

All heaven keeps the Sabbath

"All heaven is keeping the Sabbath, but not in a listless, do-nothing way. On this day every energy of the soul should be awake, for are we not to meet with God and with Christ our Saviour? We may behold Him by faith. He is longing to refresh and bless every soul" (*Counsels for the Church*, 267).

Sabbath is essential for mankind

"God saw that a Sabbath was essential for man, even in Paradise. He needed to lay aside his own interests and pursuits for one day of the seven, that he might more fully contemplate the works of God and meditate upon His power and goodness. He needed a Sabbath to remind him more vividly of God and to awaken gratitude because all that he enjoyed and possessed came from the beneficent hand of the Creator" (*Patriarchs and Prophets*, 48).

The Sabbath is a memorial of Creation

"Since the Sabbath is a memorial of the work of creation, it is a token of the love and power of Christ" (*The Desire of Ages*, 281).

The great controversy between Christ and Satan is over worship

Revelation 14:6, 7 The first angel's message is a call to worship the Creator: "Worship Him who made heaven and earth, the sea and springs of water."

Revelation 4:11 Jesus is worthy of our worship because He "created all things."

The Sabbath has an important connection to worship

Genesis 2:2 "God ended His work . . . , and rested on the seventh day."

Genesis 2:3 "God blessed the seventh day [the Sabbath] and sanctified it."

Exodus 20:8–11 "In six days the LORD made the heavens and the earth, . . . and rested the seventh day. . . . [He] blessed the Sabbath day and hallowed it." The Sabbath is a memorial of Christ's creative authority.

Luke 23:54–24:1 The order of events when Jesus was crucified: Christ

1. was crucified on Friday,
2. rested on Sabbath (Saturday) in the tomb, and
3. resurrected on Sunday.

Jesus rested in the tomb on the Sabbath of the Crucifixion weekend. His closest followers would not attend to the details of the burial until after the Sabbath, when He was already in the tomb. Worshiping God on the Sabbath was important to these believers.

Matthew 24:20	Jesus instructed His disciples to pray that their flight from Jerusalem would "not be in the winter or on the Sabbath."
Revelation 14:12	Revelation reveals an end-time remnant "who keep the commandments of God." The Sabbath is at the very heart of God's Ten Commandments.
Leviticus 23:32	Sabbath begins at sunset Friday evening. "From evening to evening, you shall celebrate your sabbath."

Elements of Sabbath worship

Psalm 100:2, 4	Worship by singing. "Come before His presence with singing." "Enter into His gates with thanksgiving, and into His courts with praise. . . . Bless His name."
Psalm 96:8	Worship by giving. "Give to the LORD the glory due His name; bring an offering, and come into His courts."
Malachi 3:10	Worship by tithing. Worship God by bringing all the tithes into the church. God will open "the windows of heaven and pour out" a blessing more abundant than what we are able to receive.
Acts 15:21	Worship by reading the Scriptures. The scriptures were being read every Sabbath.
Psalm 95:6	Worship by praying. "Oh come, let us worship and bow down; let us kneel before the LORD our Maker."
Colossians 1:27, 28	Worship by preaching. Preach Christ, "the hope of glory." (See also Luke 4:16–18.)

The Sabbath as the seal of God

| **Isaiah 8:16** | God's seal is contained in the law. |

Exodus. 20:8–11	The Sabbath commandment is in the heart of God's law and contains the characteristics of God's seal. In ancient times, a seal authenticated a legal document. It contained the name, title, and authority of the lawgiver. The Sabbath commandment has these three characteristics.
Romans 4:11	God's seal is also a sign.
Ezekiel 20:12	"I also gave them My Sabbaths, to be a sign between them and Me."
Ephesians 4:30	We are sealed by the Holy Spirit of God. The Holy Spirit impresses our hearts with Christ's love and truth so that we are settled in the truth and cannot be moved.
Revelation 7:3	God's seal is placed in our minds, as symbolized by our foreheads.
Isaiah 66:23	"From one Sabbath to another, all flesh shall come to worship before Me."

FOR FURTHER STUDY

The significance of the three angels' messages

"These truths, as presented in Revelation 14 in connection with 'the everlasting gospel,' will distinguish the church of Christ at the time of His appearing. For as the result of the threefold message it is announced: 'Here are they that keep the commandments of God, and the faith of Jesus.' And this message is the last to be given before the coming of the Lord. Immediately following its proclamation, the Son of man is seen by the prophet, coming in glory to reap the harvest of the earth" (*The Great Controversy*, 453, 454).

God's people "have been set in the world as watchmen and light bearers. To them has been entrusted the last warning for a perishing world.

On them is shining wonderful light from the word of God. They have been given a work of the most solemn import—the proclamation of the first, second, and third angels' messages. There is no other work of so great importance. They are to allow nothing else to absorb their attention" (*Testimonies for the Church*, vol. 9, 19).

Signs of Jesus' creative authority

"The duty to worship God is based upon the fact that He is the Creator and that to Him all other beings owe their existence" (*The Great Controversy*, 436).

"God Himself measured off the first week as a sample for successive weeks to the close of time. . . . It consisted of seven literal days" (*Patriarchs and Prophets*, 111).

"Had the Sabbath been universally kept, man's thoughts and affections would have been led to the Creator as the object of reverence and worship, and there would never have been an idolater, an atheist, or an infidel. The keeping of the Sabbath is a sign of loyalty to the true God" (*The Great Controversy*, 438).

The worship experience

"God is worshiped with song and music in the courts above" (*Steps to Christ*, 104).

"Both in public and in private worship it is our privilege to bow on our knees before God when we offer our petitions to Him" (*Prophets and Kings*, 48).

"There is nothing more calculated to strengthen the intellect than the study of the Scriptures. No other book is so potent to elevate the thoughts, to give vigor to the faculties, as the broad, ennobling truths of the Bible. If God's word were studied as it should be, men would have a breadth of mind, a nobility of character, and a stability of purpose rarely seen in these times" (*Steps to Christ*, 90).

Settling into the truth

"The fourth commandment alone of all the ten contains the seal of the great Lawgiver, the Creator" (*Testimonies for the Church*, vol. 6, 350).

"It is not any seal or mark that can be seen, but a settling into the truth, both intellectually and spiritually, so they cannot be moved—just as soon as God's people are sealed and prepared for the shaking, it will come" (*Last Day Events*, 219, 220).

"The seal of the living God will be placed upon those only who bear a likeness to Christ in character" (*Last Day Events*, 221).

The Sabbath will endure forever

"So long as the heavens and the earth endure, the Sabbath will continue as a sign of the Creator's power" (*The Desire of Ages*, 283).

"All heaven is keeping the Sabbath, but not in a listless, do-nothing way" (*Counsels for the Church*, 267).

Psalm 40:7, 8	Jesus' greatest delight was to do the Father's will.
Hebrews 2:9	In becoming a man, Jesus was made "a little lower than the angels" to suffer death and in death was "crowned with glory and honor."
Galatians 3:13	Christ "redeemed us from the curse of the law" by becoming "a curse for us."

The glory of the Cross

John 17:1	The hour of Christ's greatest glory was the hour of His greatest suffering.
John 17:2	In His death, Christ has triumphed over the powers of hell, and the Father has given Him "authority over all flesh." All who respond to the Spirit's leading will receive eternal life.
John 17:3	Eternal life is to know God and His Son. This "knowing" is more than intellectual knowledge. In the Bible, "to know" is to have an intimate, personal relationship with someone.
John 17:4	Christ glorified His Father and finished the work He was ordained to do.

The transfiguration

Matthew 17:1–4	Shortly before Jesus' death on the cross, His Father gave Him the assurance of His love on the Mount of Transfiguration.
Matthew 17:3	Moses, who after he died was resurrected and taken to heaven, and Elijah, who never died, spoke to Jesus about His death. (See also Luke 9:28–36.)

Matthew 17:5	At this critical moment, His Father spoke these hopeful words: "This is My beloved Son, in whom I am well pleased." These are the same words spoken at Jesus' baptism (see Matthew 3:17).
Matthew 17:6–10	Jesus instructed the disciples, "Tell the vision to no one until the Son of Man is risen from the dead." (The reason for this is that He did not want prejudice and unbelief to give an excuse for the religious leaders to put Him to death.)
Matthew 17:10–12	Jesus was soon to suffer at the hands of His enemies, and the transfiguration gave Him great encouragement and strength.

Jesus in the Garden of Gethsemane

Matthew 26:37, 38	Jesus came to Gethsemane with Peter, James, and John and asked them to wait while He prayed. "My soul is exceedingly sorrowful, even to death. Stay here and watch with Me."
Matthew 26:39	Jesus "fell on His face and prayed, saying, 'O My Father, if it is possible, let this cup pass from Me; nevertheless, not as I will, but as You will.'" Jesus gained strength to meet the coming crisis by praying in Gethsemane.
Matthew 26:40	Jesus said to His sleeping disciples, "What! Could you not watch with Me one hour?"
John 8:29	The Father was with Jesus in His suffering. Jesus said, "The Father has not left Me alone, for I always do those things that please Him."
Isaiah 52:14	Jesus' appearance revealed His internal struggle, agony, and grief over the terrible cost of sin.
Luke 22:44	Jesus in agony prayed more earnestly. "His sweat became like great drops of blood falling down to the ground."

| **Matthew 26:45, 46** | Jesus came to His disciples and said, "Are you still sleeping . . . ? Behold, the hour is at hand, and the Son of Man is being betrayed into the hands of sinners. Rise, let us be going. See, My betrayer is at hand." |
| **John 17:24** | Jesus was willing to go through the agony of Gethsemane and the death on the cross because of His desire to have us with Him through all eternity. |

FOR FURTHER STUDY

The Transfiguration

"Moses upon the mount of transfiguration was a witness to Christ's victory over sin and death. He represented those who shall come forth from the grave at the resurrection of the just. Elijah, who had been translated to heaven without seeing death, represented those who will be living upon the earth at Christ's second coming, and who will be 'changed, in a moment, in the twinkling of an eye, at the last trump;' when, 'this mortal must put on immortality,' and 'this corruptible must put on incorruption.' 1 Corinthians 15:51-53" (*The Desire of Ages*, 421, 422).

Jesus delights to do the Father's will

Jesus "stepped down from the throne, to clothe His divinity with humanity. The path from the manger to Calvary was all before His eyes. He knew the anguish that would come upon Him. He knew it all, and yet He said, 'Lo, I come: in the volume of the Book it is written of Me, I delight to do Thy will, O My God, yea, Thy law is within My heart.' Psalm 40:7, 8" (*The Desire of Ages*, 410).

Jesus' prayer is heard

"The Saviour has seen the gloom of His disciples, and has longed to lighten their grief by an assurance that their faith has not been in vain. . . . Only the three who are to witness His anguish in Gethsemane have been chosen to be with Him on the mount. . . . He pleads that they may witness a manifestation of His divinity that will comfort them in the hour of His supreme agony with the knowledge that He is of a surety the Son of God and that His shameful death is a part of the plan of redemption.

"His prayer is heard. While He is bowed in lowliness upon the stony ground, suddenly the heavens open, the golden gates of the city of God are thrown wide, and holy radiance descends upon the mount, enshrouding the Saviour's form. Divinity from within flashes through humanity, and meets the glory coming from above. Arising from His prostrate position, Christ stands in godlike majesty. The soul agony is gone. His countenance now shines 'as the sun,' and His garments are 'white as the light' " (*The Desire of Ages*, 420, 421).

Jesus' heavy burden

"With the issues of the conflict before Him, Christ's soul was filled with dread of separation from God. Satan told Him that . . . the separation would be eternal. . . .

". . . He [Jesus] came to His disciples with a yearning desire to hear some words of comfort from those whom He had so often blessed and comforted. . . . He longed to know that they were praying for Him and for themselves" (*The Desire of Ages*, 687).

"But the disciples trusted to themselves. . . . When the Savior was most in need of their sympathy and prayers, they were found asleep. . . .

"The disciples awakened at the voice of Jesus, but they hardly knew Him, His face was so changed by anguish. Addressing Peter, Jesus said, 'Simon, sleepest thou? couldest thou not watch one hour?'. . . . He did not reprove them, but said, 'Watch ye and pray, lest ye enter into temptation.' Even in His great agony, He was seeking to excuse their weakness" (*The Desire of Ages*, 688, 689).

Jesus' decision is made

"Three times has humanity shrunk from the last, crowning sacrifice. But now the history of the human race comes up before the world's Redeemer. . . . He beholds its impending fate, and His decision is made. He will save man at any cost to Himself. . . . He will not turn from His mission. He will become the propitiation of a race that has willed to sin. His prayer now breathes only submission: 'If this cup may not pass away from Me, except I drink it, Thy will be done' " (*The Desire of Ages*, 690, 693).

Jesus suffered alone, but the Father suffered with Him

"But God suffered with His Son. . . . There was silence in heaven. No harp was touched. Could mortals have viewed the amazement of the angelic host as in silent grief they watched the Father separating His beams of light, love, and glory from His beloved Son, they would better understand how offensive in His sight is sin" (*The Desire of Ages*, 693).

The angel Gabriel was with Christ in the garden

"The worlds unfallen and the heavenly angels had watched with intense interest as the conflict drew to its close. . . . Angels had longed to bring relief to the divine sufferer, but this might not be. . . . The mighty angel who stands in God's presence . . . came to the side of Christ. The angel came not to take the cup from Christ's hand, but to strengthen Him to drink it, with the assurance of the Father's love. . . . He told Him that He would see of the travail of His soul, and be satisfied, for He would see a multitude of the human race saved, eternally saved" (*The Desire of Ages*, 693, 694).

Jesus meets His betrayer

"No traces of His recent agony were visible as Jesus stepped forth to meet His betrayer. . . . A divine light illuminated the Saviour's face, and a dovelike form overshadowed Him. In the presence of this divine glory, the murderous throng could not stand for a moment. They staggered back. Priests, elders, soldiers, and Judas fell as dead men to the ground.

". . . Jesus had opportunity to escape, but He remained, calm and self-possessed" (*The Desire of Ages*, 694).

John 8:29	Jesus has confidence in His Father's continual presence in His life. He said, "He who sent Me is with Me. The Father has not left Me alone, for I always do those things that please Him."
Matthew 26:45, 46	With the divine assurance of the Father's presence, Jesus was now ready to face the mob. He said, "The Son of Man is being betrayed into the hands of sinners."
Matthew 26:47–50	Judas came with religious leaders and identified Jesus by kissing Him. Then the guards took Him.
John 16:32	Jesus had predicted that the disciples would flee at the time of His greatest trial. "The hour is coming, yes, has now come, that you will be scattered, each to his own, and will leave Me alone. And yet I am not alone, because the Father is with Me."
Luke 22:54	Jesus, the divine Son of God, the One who will judge all, was arrested and interrogated by the high priest.
Luke 22:55–62	Peter denied Jesus three times. With divine insight, Jesus had also predicted Peter's denial: "Before the rooster crows, you will deny Me three times. So Peter went out and wept bitterly."
Luke 22:63–65	Human beings created in the image of God so defiled that image that they mocked and beat their Creator. They blindfolded Him, struck Him on the face, and cynically asked Him to tell them who struck Him.

Luke 22:66, 67	The Jewish religious leaders urged Him to reveal whether He was the Christ. They did not do this because they sincerely wanted to know but because they wanted further evidence to condemn Him.
Luke 22:67	Knowing their intent, Jesus said: "If I tell you, you will by no means believe."
Luke 22:69	Jesus then revealed His majesty by declaring: "Hereafter the Son of Man will sit on the right hand of the power of God."
Luke 22:70	They asked Him again: "Are You then the Son of God?" Jesus answered, "You rightly say that I am."
Luke 22:71	They said: "What further testimony do we need? For we have heard it ourselves from His own mouth."

Pilate's first compromise

Luke 23:1–5	The crowd took Him to Pilate, and he asked Jesus: " 'Are You the King of the Jews?' "He answered him and said, 'It is as you say.' "
Luke 23:6, 7	As soon as Pilate learned that Jesus was a Galilean, he sent Him to Herod.
Luke 23:11	Herod treated Jesus with contempt, mocked Him, clothed "Him in a gorgeous robe, and sent Him back to Pilate."

Pilate's second compromise

Luke 23:13–14	Pilate examined Jesus and claimed, "I have found no fault in this Man concerning those things of which you accuse Him."
Luke 23:15, 16	Neither Herod nor Pilate found any fault in Him. Pilate said, "Nothing deserving of death has been done by Him. I will therefore chastise Him, and release Him."

Pilate's third compromise

Luke 23:15–17 It was a Roman custom to release one Jewish prisoner at the feast of the Passover. Pilate offered the Jews either Christ or Barabbas.

Luke 23:18, 19 Amazingly, the crowd chose Barabbas. They shouted, "Away with this Man, and release to us Barabbas."

Luke 23:20–22 Pilate wanted to release Jesus, but the crowd asked that He be crucified. Pilate, for the third time, appealed to them: "Why, what evil has He done? I have found no reason for death in Him. I will therefore chastise Him and let Him go."

Luke 23:23–25 "They were insistent, demanding with loud voices that He be crucified," so Pilate sentenced Jesus as they requested. He released Barabbas to them.

Those who crucified Jesus will see Him when He returns as King of kings

Revelation 1:7 "Behold He is coming with clouds, and every eye shall see Him, even they who pierced Him. And all the tribes of the earth will mourn because of Him."

Revelation 19:16 Jesus returns to earth at His second coming as King of kings and Lord of Lords.

FOR FURTHER STUDY

The glory of Jesus revealed

"Jesus had opportunity to escape, but He remained, calm and self-possessed. As one glorified He stood in the midst of that hardened band, now prostrate and helpless at His feet. The disciples looked on, silent with wonder and awe" (*The Desire of Ages*, 694).

Jesus on trial

"Pilate looked at the men who had Jesus in charge, and then his gaze rested searchingly on Jesus. He had had to deal with all kinds of criminals; but never before had a man bearing marks of such goodness and nobility been brought before him. On His face he saw no sign of guilt, no expression of fear, no boldness or defiance. He saw a man of calm and dignified bearing, whose countenance bore not the marks of a criminal, but the signature of heaven.

"Christ's appearance made a favorable impression upon Pilate. His better nature was roused. He had heard of Jesus and His works. . . . He resolved to demand of the Jews their charges against the prisoner" (*The Desire of Ages*, 724).

"Herod promised that if Christ would perform some miracle in his presence, He should be released. Christ's accusers had seen with their own eyes the mighty works wrought by His power. They had heard Him command the grave to give up its dead. They had seen the dead come forth obedient to His voice. Fear seized them lest He should now work a miracle. Of all things they most dreaded an exhibition of His power. Such a manifestation would prove a deathblow to their plans, and would perhaps cost them their lives" (*The Desire of Ages*, 729, 730).

"Pilate's face grew pale. He was confused by his own conflicting emotions. But while he had been delaying to act, the priests and rulers were still further inflaming the minds of the people. Pilate was forced to action. He now bethought himself of a custom which might serve to secure Christ's release. . . . The Roman authorities at this time held a prisoner named Barabbas, who was under sentence of death. This man had claimed to be the Messiah. He claimed authority to establish a different order of things, to set the world right. . . . Pilate thought to arouse them to a sense of justice. He hoped to gain their sympathy for Jesus in opposition to the priests and rulers. So, turning to the crowd, he said with great earnestness, 'Whom will ye that I release unto you? Barabbas, or Jesus which is called Christ?' " (*The Desire of Ages*, 733).

"Pilate yielded to the demands of the mob. Rather than risk losing his position, he delivered Jesus up to be crucified" (*The Desire of Ages*, 738).

Christ will return in glory

"When Christ shall come to the earth again, not as a prisoner surrounded by a rabble will men see Him. They will see Him then as heaven's King. Christ will come in His own glory, in the glory of His Father, and the glory of the holy angels. Ten thousand times ten thousand, and thousands of thousands of angels, the beautiful and triumphant sons of God, possessing surpassing loveliness and glory, will escort Him on His way. Then shall He sit upon the throne of His glory, and before Him shall be gathered all nations. Then every eye shall see Him, and they also that pierced Him. In the place of a crown of thorns, He will wear a crown of glory,—a crown within a crown. In place of that old purple kingly robe, He will be clothed in raiment of whitest white, 'so as no fuller on earth can white them.' Mark 9:3. And on His vesture and on His thigh a name will be written, 'King of kings, and Lord of lords.' Revelation 19:16" (*The Desire of Ages*, 739).

John 12:32	Jesus promised, "And I, if I am lifted up from the earth, will draw all peoples to Myself."
Matthew 27:11	Pilate pressed Jesus regarding His identity by asking, " 'Are You the King of the Jews?' "Jesus said to him, 'It is as you say.' "
Matthew 27:15–21	Pilate offered to release either Barabbas or Jesus. The mob chose a well-known, hardened criminal over the caring, compassionate Jesus.
Matthew 27:22, 23	"Pilate said to them, 'What then shall I do with Jesus who is called Christ?' " They screamed, "Let Him be crucified!"
Matthew 27:24	Compromising Pilate saw he could not influence the crowd to free Jesus, so he washed his hands before the multitude, saying, "I am innocent of the blood of this just Person."
Matthew 27:25	The people shouted, "His blood be on us and on our children." They pronounced sentence upon themselves. The Messiah had come, and they failed to recognize Him.
Matthew 27:26	Pilate released Barabbas, scourged Jesus, and delivered Him to be crucified.
Matthew 27:27–31	Roman soldiers mistreated Jesus. They stripped Him to the waist, clothed Him with a scarlet robe, placed a crown of twisted thorns on His head, and put a reed in His right hand. Then they mocked Him, calling Him King of the Jews. They then crucified Him. He suffered it all, enduring the shame, ridicule, and mockery to redeem us.

Prophesies fulfilled at Christ's crucifixion

Psalm 55:12, 13   Jesus would be betrayed by a friend. See the fulfillment with Judas in Matthew 26:47–50.

Zechariah 11:12, 13   Jesus would be betrayed for thirty pieces of silver. See the fulfillment in Matthew 26:14–16.

Isaiah 53:4–7   Jesus would be led as a lamb to the slaughter. See the fulfillment in Matthew 27:22–31; see also Acts 8:32–35.

Isaiah 53:3   "He is despised and rejected of men,
A Man of sorrows and acquainted with grief.
And we hid, as it were, our faces from Him;
He was despised, and we did not esteem Him."
See the fulfillment in John 1:11, Luke 23:18.

Psalm 22:16, 17   Prophecy said the Messiah's hands and feet would be pierced with nails. He was to be crucified and not stoned. See the fulfillment in Luke 23:33.

Psalm 22:18   They would cast lots for His clothing. See the fulfillment in Matthew 27:35.

Psalm 34:20   Not one of His bones would be broken. See the fulfillment in John 19:33.

Psalm 22:1   "My God, My God, why have You forsaken Me?" See Matthew 27:46.

Isaiah 53:9   Jesus would be buried in a rich man's tomb. See the fulfillment in Matthew 27:57–60.

Psalm 16:10   Jesus would rise from the dead. See the fulfillment in Matthew 28:1–7.

Christ on the cross

Luke 23:34   Jesus said, "Father, forgive them, for they do not know what they do."

Matthew 27:37   "They nailed a placard with the accusation written against Him: 'This is Jesus the King of the Jews.' "

Matthew 27:40	Some people challenged Him, "You who destroy the temple and build it in three days, save Yourself! If You are the Son of God, come down from the cross."
Matthew 27:41–43	The religious leaders mocked Him by saying, "He saved others; Himself He cannot save. If He is the King of Israel, let Him now come down from the cross, and we will believe Him."
Luke 23:42, 43	In one of His last acts of mercy, Jesus gave a dying thief the assurance of eternal life.

The seven sayings of Christ from the cross

John 19:27	Jesus revealed His care for His mother when he said to John, "Behold your Mother."
John 19:28	Jesus revealed His humanity when He said, "I thirst!"
Luke 23:34	Jesus revealed the wonder of grace when He said, "Father, forgive them, for they know not what they do."
Luke 23:43	Jesus revealed the reality of eternal life when He said to a dying thief, "You will be with Me in Paradise."
Matthew 27:46	Jesus revealed the enormity of sin when He cried out, "My God, My God, why have You forsaken Me?"
John 19:30	Jesus revealed the assurance of our salvation when He said, "It is finished."
Luke 23:46	Jesus revealed His faith when He said, "Father, into Your hands I commit My spirit."

Jesus' final words at the end of time

Revelation 16:17	"It is done." The plan of salvation is complete, and victory for God's people is certain.

Jesus' appearance

"The Saviour made no murmur of complaint. His face remained calm and serene, but great drops of sweat stood upon His brow. There was no pitying hand to wipe the death dew from His face, nor words of sympathy and unchanging fidelity to stay His human heart" (*The Desire of Ages*, 744).

Jesus prayed for His enemies

"While the soldiers were doing their fearful work, Jesus prayed for His enemies, 'Father forgive them; for they know not what they do.' . . . No curses were called down upon the soldiers who were handling Him so roughly. No vengeance was invoked upon the priests and rulers, who were gloating over the accomplishment of their purpose. Christ pitied them in their ignorance and guilt" (*The Desire of Ages*, 744).

Christ's suffering at Calvary

"As soon as Jesus was nailed to the cross, it was lifted by strong men, and with great violence thrust into the place prepared for it. This caused the most intense agony to the Son of God" (*The Desire of Ages*, 745).

"The priests saw what they had done, and asked Pilate to change the inscription. They said, 'Write not, The King of the Jews; but that He said, I am King of the Jews.' . . .

"A higher power than Pilate or the Jews had directed the placing of that inscription above the head of Jesus" (*The Desire of Ages*, 745).

"Jesus, suffering and dying, heard every word as the priests declared, 'He saved others; Himself He cannot save. Let Christ the King of Israel descend now from the cross, that we may see and believe.' Christ could have come down from the cross. But it is because He would not save Himself that the sinner has hope of pardon and favor with God. . . .

". . . Those who in derision uttered the words, 'He trusted in God; let Him deliver Him now, if He will have Him: for He said, I am the Son of God,' little thought that their testimony would sound down the ages. . . . These words led men to search the Scriptures as they had never done before. . . . Never before was there such a general knowledge of Jesus as when He hung upon the cross" (*The Desire of Ages*, 749).

The thief's background

"This man was not a hardened criminal; he had been led astray by evil associations. . . . He had seen and heard Jesus, and had been convicted by His teaching, but he had been turned away from Him by the priests and rulers. . . . In the judgment hall and on the way to Calvary he had been in company with Jesus. . . .

". . . The Holy Spirit illuminates his mind. . . . In Jesus, . . . hanging upon the cross, he sees the Lamb of God, that taketh away the sin of the world" (*The Desire of Ages*, 749, 750).

Christ's promise to the thief

"Christ did not promise that the thief should be with Him in Paradise that day. He Himself did not go that day to Paradise. He slept in the tomb, and on the morning of the resurrection He said, 'I am not yet ascended to My Father.' John 20:17. But on the day of the crucifixion, the day of apparent defeat and darkness, the promise was given. 'Today' while dying upon the cross as a malefactor, Christ assures the poor sinner, Thou shalt be with Me in Paradise" (*The Desire of Ages*, 751).

Justified by His righteousness

"Christ was treated as we deserve, that we might be treated as He deserves. He was condemned for our sins, in which He had no share, that we might be justified by His righteousness, in which we had no share. He suffered the death which was ours, that we might receive the life which was His. 'With His stripes we are healed' " (*The Desire of Ages*, 25).

Jesus' commitment to our salvation

"Now with the terrible weight of guilt He bears, He cannot see the Father's reconciling face. . . .

". . . The Saviour could not see through the portals of the tomb. Hope did not present to Him His coming forth from the grave a conqueror, or tell Him of the Father's acceptance of the sacrifice. He feared that sin was so offensive to God that Their separation was to be eternal" (*The Desire of Ages*, 753).

Jesus trusts the Father's love

"A light encircled the cross, and the face of the Saviour shone with a glory like the sun. He then bowed His head upon His breast, and died.

". . . In those dreadful hours He had relied upon the evidence of His Father's acceptance heretofore given Him. . . . By faith He rested in Him whom it had ever been His joy to obey" (*The Desire of Ages*, 756).

Jesus humbles Himself

"It was the marvel of all the universe that Christ should humble Himself to save fallen man. . . . When Christ came to our world in the form of humanity, all were intensely interested in following Him as He traversed, step by step, the bloodstained path from the manger to Calvary" (*Patriarchs and Prophets*, 69).

The fulfillment of "It is finished" at the end of time

"It is at midnight that God manifests His power for the deliverance of His people. . . . In the midst of the angry heavens is one clear space of indescribable glory, whence comes the voice of God like the sound of many waters, saying: 'It is done' " (*The Great Controversy*, 636).

"The voice of God is heard from heaven, declaring the day and hour of Jesus' coming, and delivering the everlasting covenant to His people. . . .

". . . Soon there appears in the east a small black cloud about half the size of a man's hand. It is the cloud which surrounds the Saviour and which seems in the distance to be shrouded in darkness. The people of God know this to be the sign of the Son of man. . . . Jesus rides forth as a mighty conqueror" (*The Great Controversy*, 640, 641).

"It was Satan's purpose to bring about an eternal separation between God and man; but in Christ we become more closely united to God than if we had never fallen" (*The Desire of Ages*, 25).

Jesus' death assures Satan's destruction

"The death of Christ upon the cross made sure the destruction of him who has the power of death, who was the originator of sin" (*Signs of the Times*, December 30, 1889, 2).

"Through Christ's redeeming work the government of God stands justified. . . . Rebellion can never again arise. Sin can never again enter the universe. Through eternal ages all are secure from apostasy. By love's self-sacrifice, the inhabitants of earth and heaven are bound to their Creator in bonds of indissoluble union" (*The Desire of Ages*, 26).

Jesus wins! Satan loses!

14

Jesus' Victory Over Death

Revelation 1:18 The grave can no longer hold its victims captive because Jesus has triumphed over death. Jesus said, "I am He who lives, and was dead, and behold, I am alive forevermore. Amen. And I have the keys of Hades and of Death."

Revelation 20:6 Since Christ was resurrected from the dead, we need not fear death. He promises, "Blessed and holy is he who has part in the first resurrection."

Revelation 21:4 One day, death will be defeated forever. God will wipe away every tear from our eyes; "there shall be no more death, nor sorrow, nor crying. There shall be no more pain."

1 Corinthians 15:20 "Christ is risen from the dead, and has become the firstfruits of those who have fallen asleep."

1 Corinthians 15:21–23 Death came to man through sin, but through Christ "came the resurrection of the dead. For as in Adam all die, even so in Christ all shall be made alive."

Genesis 3:15 In Eden, God gave Adam and Eve the first promise of victory.

Romans 6:23 "The wages of sin is death, but the gift of God is eternal life in Christ."

What happens when we die?

Genesis 2:7 "And the Lord God formed man of the dust of the ground, and breathed into his nostrils the breath of life; and man became a living soul" (KJV). The soul is not some immortal consciousness that God breathed into us.

Matthew 16:26	One meaning of the word *soul* in the Bible is "life." "What is a man profited, if he shall gain the whole world, and lose his own soul?" (KJV).
1 Corinthians 15:51, 52	"We shall not all sleep, but we shall all be changed, . . . at the last trump: . . . the dead shall be raised incorruptible" (KJV). In the Bible, the dead are asleep until the resurrection at the Second Coming.
Ecclesiastes 12:7	At death "shall the dust return to the earth as it was: and the spirit shall return unto God who gave it" (KJV).
Psalm 146:4	The spirit departs back to God, the person returns to dust, and man's plans (thoughts) perish.
Job 27:3	In the Bible, the "breath of life" that God breathes into human beings is also called "God's spirit." It is His life-giving power.
Ecclesiastes 9:5	"The living know that they will die, but the dead know nothing."

Jesus' power over death

Luke 7:13–15	Jesus demonstrates His power over death in the resurrection of the widow of Nain's son.
Mark 5:22, 23	When Jairus, a ruler of the synagogue, saw Jesus, "he fell at His feet and begged Him earnestly, saying, 'My little daughter lies at the point of death. Come and lay Your hands on her, that she may be healed, and she will live.' "
Mark 5:35–39	People from the ruler's house told Jairus it was too late to ask Jesus for help because his daughter had already died. Jesus encouraged Jairus to "only believe," and he would experience His miracle-working power.

Mark 5:40–42	Jesus entered where the child was lying and took the twelve-year-old girl "by the hand, and said to her, 'Little girl, I say to you, arise.' Immediately the girl arose and walked. . . . And they were overcome with great amazement."
John 11:1–10	Another example of Jesus' understanding of death and His power over it is the resurrection of Lazarus. Mary and Martha sent Jesus the message, " 'Lord, behold, he whom You love is sick.'
	"When Jesus heard that, He said, 'This sickness is not unto death, but for the glory of God, that the Son of God may be glorified through it.' " Jesus delayed going. Lazarus died.
John 11:11–15	Jesus told his disciples, "Our friend Lazarus sleeps, but I go that I may wake him up." His disciples said, "Lord, if he sleeps, he will get well." However, Jesus referred to his death. Then Jesus told them clearly, "Lazarus is dead."
John 11:17–22	When Jesus came, He found that Lazarus was dead already and had been in the tomb four days.
John 11:23–26	Jesus said to Martha, "Your brother will rise again." Martha replied, "I know that he will rise again in the resurrection at the last day." Jesus declared, "I am the resurrection and the life. He who believes in Me, though he may die, he shall live. And whoever lives and believes in Me shall never die. Do you believe this?"
John 11:40–42	Jesus said, "Did I not say to you that if you would believe you would see the glory of God?" At Lazarus's tomb, in faith, Jesus prayed a prayer of thanksgiving before He raised Lazarus from the dead.

| John 11:43–45 | "He [Jesus] cried with a loud voice, 'Lazarus, come forth!' And he who had died came out bound hand and foot with graveclothes. . . . Jesus said to them, 'Loose him, and let him go.' " As a result of Lazarus's resurrection, many believed in Jesus. |

The blessed hope

Titus 2:13	"Looking for the blessed hope and glorious appearing of our great God and Savior Jesus Christ, who gave Himself for us."
1 Thessalonians 4:16	The dead in Christ will rise first.
Isaiah 25:8; Revelation 21:3, 4	Jesus will defeat death forever. And the Lord God will wipe away the tears from all faces.

FOR FURTHER STUDY

Christ is the firstfruits

"Christ the first fruits represented the great spiritual harvest to be gathered for the kingdom of God. His resurrection is the type and pledge of the resurrection of all the righteous dead. . . .

"To the believer, Christ is the resurrection and the life. . . . The life that He laid down in humanity, He takes up again, and gives to humanity" (*The Desire of Ages*, 786, 787).

Jesus miraculously raises the dead

The widow of Nain. "He who stood beside the sorrowing mother at the gate of Nain, watches with every mourning one beside the bier. He is touched with sympathy for our grief. . . . His word, that called the dead to life, is no less efficacious now than when spoken to the young man of Nain. He says, 'All power is given unto Me in heaven and in earth.' Matthew 28:18. That power is not diminished by the lapse of years, nor exhausted by the ceaseless activity of His overflowing grace. To all who believe on Him He is still a living Saviour. . . .

"Satan cannot hold the dead in his grasp when the Son of God bids them live" (*The Desire of Ages*, 319, 320).

The resurrection of Lazarus. "Lazarus had been laid in a cave in a rock, and a massive stone had been placed before the entrance. 'Take ye away the stone,' Christ said. Thinking that He only wished to look upon the dead, Martha objected, saying that the body had been buried four days, and corruption had already begun its work. This statement, made before the raising of Lazarus, left no room for Christ's enemies to say that a deception had been practiced. . . . When Christ raised to life the daughter of Jairus, He had said, 'The damsel is not dead, but sleepeth.' Mark 5:39. As she had been sick only a short time, and was raised immediately after death, the Pharisees declared that the child had not been dead; that Christ Himself had said she was only asleep. They had tried to make it appear that Christ could not cure disease, that there was foul play about His miracles. But in this case, none could deny that Lazarus was dead" (*The Desire of Ages*, 534, 535).

"In delaying to come to Lazarus, Christ had a purpose of mercy toward those who had not received Him. He tarried, that by raising Lazarus from the dead He might give to His stubborn, unbelieving people another evidence that he was indeed 'the resurrection, and the life.' . . . This crowning miracle, the raising of Lazarus, was to set the seal of God on His work and on His claim to divinity" (*The Desire of Ages*, 529).

"Lazarus is set free, and stands before the company, not as one emaciated from disease, and with feeble, tottering limbs, but as a man in the prime of life, and in the vigor of a noble manhood. His eyes beam with intelligence and with love for his Saviour. He casts himself in adoration at the feet of Jesus" (*The Desire of Ages*, 536).

The righteous dead are resurrected. "All come forth from their graves the same in stature as when they entered the tomb. Adam, who stands among the risen throng, is of lofty height and majestic form, in stature but little below the Son of God. He presents a marked contrast to the people of later generations; in this one respect is shown the great degeneracy of the race. But all arise with the freshness and vigor of eternal youth. . . . All blemishes and deformities are left in the grave. Restored to the tree of life in the long-lost Eden, the redeemed will 'grow up' (Malachi 4:2) to the full stature of the race in its primeval glory. . . . Oh, wonderful redemption! long talked of, long hoped for, contemplated with eager anticipation, but never fully understood.

". . . Friends long separated by death are united, nevermore to part, and with songs of gladness ascend together to the City of God" (*The Great Controversy*, 644, 645).

"The voice of the Son of God is heard calling forth the sleeping saints, and as the prophet beholds them coming from the prison house of death, he exclaims, 'Thy dead men shall live, together with my dead body shall they arise. Awake and sing, ye that dwell in dust; for thy dew is as the dew of herbs, and the earth shall cast out the dead.' . . .

"In the visions of the prophet, those who have triumphed over sin and the grave are now seen happy in the presence of their Maker, talking freely with Him as man talked with God in the beginning" (*Prophets and Kings*, 728, 729).

Jesus won the victory over death!

15

Jesus' Resurrection

The resurrection of Christ proves His victory over the grave

John 2:19	Jesus predicted His death and resurrection. "Destroy this temple, and in three days I will raise it up."
Matthew 17:22, 23	Jesus said to His disciples, "The Son of Man is about to be betrayed into the hands of men, and they will kill Him, and the third day He will be raised up."
Matthew 28:1	Mary Magdalene and the other Mary found the tomb empty when they came to embalm His body.
Mark 16:3, 4	"They said among themselves, 'Who will roll away the stone from the door of the tomb for us?' But when they looked up, they saw that the stone had been rolled away—for it was very large."
Matthew 28:2–4	"An angel of the Lord descended from heaven, and came and rolled back the stone from the door, and sat on it. His countenance was like lightning, and his clothing as white as snow. And the guards shook for fear of him, and became like dead men."
Matthew 28:5–8	"The angel . . . said to the women, 'Do not be afraid, for I know that you seek Jesus who was crucified. He is not here; for He is risen.' " Then he asked them to share the news with the disciples.
John 20:14–16	Mary stayed at the tomb weeping and wondering what had happened to the body of Jesus. Jesus appeared to her and asked, "Woman, why are you weeping? Whom are you seeking?" She mistook him for the gardener until He called her by her name.

John 20:17	"Jesus said to her, 'Do not cling to Me, for I have not yet ascended to My Father, but go to My brethren and say to them, "I am ascending to My Father and your Father, and to My God and your God." ' "
Matthew 28:9, 10	When the women went to tell Jesus' disciples that He had risen, Jesus met them and said, "Do not be afraid. Go and tell My brethren to go to Galilee, and there they will see Me."
Luke 24:13–35	Jesus met two of His disciples on the road to Emmaus, but they didn't recognize Him. He gave them a Bible study on the Messianic prophecies from the Old Testament. At supper, they recognized who He was. They ran to tell the rest of the disciples.
Luke 24:36	As these two disciples shared their story with the larger group, Jesus appeared to them.
Luke 24:45–48	Jesus "opened their understanding, that they might comprehend the Scriptures."
Luke 24:49	"I send the Promise of My Father upon you; but tarry in the city of Jerusalem until you are endued with power from on high."

Scriptures' hopeful message regarding Jesus' resurrection

1 Corinthians 15:20	"Christ is risen from the dead, and has become the firstfruits of those who have fallen asleep."
John 10:17, 18	"My Father loves Me, because I lay down My life that I may take it again. No one takes it from Me, but I lay it down of Myself. I have power to lay it down, and I have power to take it again. This command I have received from My Father."
Hebrews 7:25	Jesus lives eternally to intercede for us.

An angel rolled away the stone

"A young man clothed in shining garments was sitting by the tomb. It was the angel who had rolled away the stone. He had taken the guise of humanity that he might not alarm these friends of Jesus" (*The Desire of Ages*, 788, 789).

"The face they look upon is not the face of mortal warrior; it is the face of the mightiest of the Lord's host. This messenger is he who fills the position from which Satan fell. . . . The soldiers see him removing the stone as he would a pebble, and hear him cry, Son of God, come forth; Thy Father calls Thee. They see Jesus come forth from the grave, and hear Him proclaim over the rent sepulcher, 'I am the resurrection, and the life' " (*The Desire of Ages*, 779, 780).

Roman soldiers become like dead men

"At sight of the angels and the glorified Saviour the Roman guards had fainted and become as dead men" (*The Desire of Ages*, 781).

The angel's voice at the tomb

"When the voice of the mighty angel was heard at Christ's tomb, saying Thy Father calls Thee, the Savior came forth from the grave by the life that was in Himself" (*The Desire of Ages*, 785).

Jesus is risen

"He is risen, He is risen! The women repeat the words again and again. No need now for the anointing spices. The Saviour is living, and not dead. They remember now that when speaking of His death He said that He would rise again. What a day is this to the world! Quickly the women departed from the sepulcher 'with fear and great joy; and did run to bring His disciples word' " (*The Desire of Ages*, 789).

On the road to Emmaus

"Had the disciples failed to press their invitation, they would not have known that their traveling companion was the risen Lord. Christ never forces His company upon anyone. He interests Himself in those who need Him. Gladly will He enter the humblest home, and cheer the lowliest heart. But if men are too indifferent to think of the heavenly Guest, or ask Him to abide with them, He passes on. Thus many meet with great loss" (*The Desire of Ages*, 800).

"Beginning at Moses, . . . Christ expounded in all the Scriptures the things concerning Himself. . . . It was necessary for them to understand the witness borne to Him by the types and prophecies of the Old Testament. Upon these their faith must be established. . . .

"In teaching these disciples, Jesus showed the importance of the Old Testament as a witness to His mission. Many professed Christians now discard the Old Testament, claiming that it is no longer of any use. But such is not Christ's teaching" (*The Desire of Ages*, 796, 799).

His disciples recognize Him

"The simple evening meal of bread is soon prepared. . . . He puts forth His hands to bless the food. The disciples start back in astonishment. Their companion spreads forth His hands in the same way as their Master used to do. They look again, and lo, they see in His hands the print of nails. Both exclaim at once. It is the Lord Jesus! He has risen from the dead!

". . . They leave their meal untasted, and full of joy immediately set out again on the same path by which they came, hurrying to tell the tidings to the disciples in the city. . . .

". . . They no longer mourn over Him as dead. Christ is risen— repeatedly they repeat it" (*The Desire of Ages*, 800, 801).

Hope for the righteous dead

"The precious dead, from Adam down to the last saint who dies, will hear the voice of the Son of God, and will come forth from the grave to immortal life. God will be their God, and they shall be His people. There will be a close and tender relationship between God and the risen saints" (*The Desire of Ages*, 606).

Jesus' Ascension

John 14:28	Jesus told His disciples He would go to the Father. He said, " 'I am going to the Father,' for My Father is greater than I."
John 14:29	Jesus said to His disciples, "Now I have told you before it comes, that when it does come to pass, you may believe."
Matthew 28:20	Jesus promised His disciples as He was about to ascend back to His throne of glory that He would be with them always.
Luke 24:49	Jesus gave the disciples the Promise of His Father but asked them to tarry in the city of Jerusalem until they received power from on high.
Acts 2:33	Jesus was "exalted to the right hand of God" and "received from the Father the promise of the Holy Spirit," then He poured out the Holy Spirit on the disciples.
Luke 24:53	The disciples waited in Jerusalem for the promise of the outpouring of the Holy Spirit, but they did not wait in idleness. They were "continually in the temple praising and blessing God."
Acts 1:8	When the Holy Spirit came upon them, then they were witnesses of Jesus.

Jesus' three promises to His disciples

John 14:16–18 Jesus promised His disciples that He would pray to the Father, and He would give them another Helper, that He—the Spirit of Truth—would abide with them forever. He said, "I will not leave you orphans; I will come to you."

John 15:26 Jesus told His disciples that the Helper (the Holy Spirit) would come from the Father and would testify of Him.

Acts 1:4–8 Jesus said for the disciples to wait for the Promise of the Father. He told them, "John truly baptized with water, but you shall be baptized with the Holy Spirit not many days from now." . . . "You shall receive power when the Holy Spirit has come upon you; and you shall be witnesses to Me in Jerusalem, and in all Judea and Samaria, and to the end of the earth."

Acts 2:1–4 The Holy Spirit was poured out in abundant measure on the Day of Pentecost. "When the Day of Pentecost had fully come, they were all with one accord in one place. . . . And they were all filled with the Holy Spirit and began to speak with other tongues, as the Spirit gave them utterance."

1 Corinthians 12:7, 11 "The manifestation of the Spirit is given to each one for the profit of all." The Holy Spirit distributes the gifts "to each one individually as He wills."

Ephesians 4:7 "To each one of us grace was given according to the measure of Christ's gift."

Ephesians 4:8 When Jesus ascended to heaven, He gave gifts to men.

Ephesians 4:11–15 The Holy Spirit chose "some to be apostles, some prophets, some evangelists, and some pastors and teachers, for the equipping of the saints for the work of ministry, for the edifying of the body of Christ . . . ; that we should no longer be children, tossed to and fro and carried about with every wind of doctrine, by the trickery of men, in the cunning craftiness of deceitful plotting, but, speaking the truth in love, may grow up in all things into Him who is the head—Christ."

The promise of the second coming of Christ

Acts 1:9–11 The disciples were watching as Jesus ascended to heaven in a cloud. "While they looked steadfastly toward heaven . . . , two men stood by them in white apparel, who also said, 'Men of Galilee, why do you stand gazing up into heaven? This same Jesus, who was taken up from you into heaven, will come in like manner as you saw Him go into heaven.' "

Song the angels sang at Christ's ascension

Psalm 24:7–10 "Lift up your heads, O ye gates; . . .
And the King of glory shall come in.
Who is this King of glory?
The LORD strong and mighty. . . .
The LORD of hosts;
He is the King of glory."

Hebrews 1:6 The Father's arms encircled His Son, and the word was given, "Let all the angels of God worship Him."

Revelation 5:12, 13 "Ten thousand times ten thousand, and thousands of thousands" of angels sang:

'Blessing and honor and glory and power
Be to Him who sits on the throne,
And to the Lamb, forever and ever!' "

Hebrews 7:25	Jesus is able to save "those who come to God through Him." He lives to make intercession for us.
Hebrews 4:16	Everyone can come to the throne of grace to obtain mercy and find grace in time of need.

Jesus requests that His earthly children be with Him

John 17:24	When Jesus embraced the Father in heaven after being gone for thirty-three and a half years, He waved the heavenly host back until He presented His request to the Father. He had previously prayed, "Father, I desire that they also whom You gave Me may be with Me where I am, that they may behold My glory which You have given Me."

FOR FURTHER STUDY

Jesus' promise

"Christ had sojourned in the world for thirty-three years; He had endured its scorn, insult, and mockery; He had been rejected and crucified. Now, when about to ascend to His throne of glory,—as He reviews the ingratitude of the people He came to save,—will He not withdraw from them His sympathy and love? Will not His affections be centered upon that realm where He is appreciated. . . ? No; His promise to those loved ones whom He leaves on earth is, 'I am with you alway, even unto the end of the world' " (*The Desire of Ages*, 830).

The disciples wait for the right time and place

"In obedience to Christ's command, [the disciples] waited in Jerusalem for the promise of the Father—the outpouring of the Spirit. They did not wait in idleness. The record says that they were 'continually in the temple, praising and blessing God' " (*The Acts of the Apostles*, 35).

"They also met together to present their requests to the Father in the name of Jesus. They knew that they had a Representative in heaven, an Advocate at the throne of God" (*The Acts of the Apostles*, 35, 36).

The disciples wait for the right experience

"As the disciples waited for the fulfillment of the promise, they humbled their hearts in true repentance and confessed their unbelief. . . .

". . . Putting away all differences, all desire for the supremacy, they came close together in Christian fellowship" (*The Acts of the Apostles*, 36, 37).

Pentecost: The outpouring of the Holy Spirit

"The Savior was pointing forward to the time when the Holy Spirit should come to do a mighty work as His representative. . . .

". . . What was the result of the outpouring of the Spirit on the Day of Pentecost? The glad tidings of a risen Saviour were carried to the uttermost parts of the inhabited world" (*The Acts of the Apostles*, 47, 48).

"After Christ's ascension His enthronement in His mediatorial kingdom was signalized by the outpouring of the Holy Spirit. On the day of Pentecost the Spirit was given. Christ's witnesses proclaimed the power of the risen Saviour" (*Christ's Object Lessons*, 120). The Holy Spirit was poured out on the Day of Pentecost as a signal to the early church that Jesus' sacrifice was accepted by the Father in the heavenly sanctuary. This was heaven's gift that Jesus' sacrifice on Calvary's cross was complete.

Signal to receive the promised blessing

"Christ's ascension to heaven was the signal that His followers were to receive the promised blessing. . . . As soon as this ceremony was completed, the Holy Spirit descended upon the disciples in rich currents, and Christ was indeed glorified, even with the glory which He had with the Father from all eternity. The Pentecostal outpouring was Heaven's communication that the Redeemer's inauguration was accomplished" (*The Acts of the Apostles*, 38, 39).

Multitude raised

"As Christ arose, He brought from the grave a multitude of captives. . . .

". . . Those who came forth from the grave at Christ's resurrection were raised to everlasting life. They ascended with Him as trophies of His victory over death and the grave. These, said Christ, are no longer the captives of Satan; I have redeemed them" (*The Desire of Ages*, 786).

"The same power that raised Christ from the dead will raise His church, and glorify it with Him, above all principalities, above all powers, above every name that is named, not only in this world, but also in the world to come" (*The Desire of Ages*, 787).

The angels greet Christ with song

"As they drew near to the city of God, the challenge is given by the escorting angels,—

'Lift up your heads, O ye gates;
And be ye lift up, ye everlasting doors;
And the King of glory shall come in.'

"Joyfully the waiting sentinels respond,—

'Who is this King of glory?'

"This they say, not because they know not who He is, but because they would hear the answer of exalted praise,—

'The Lord strong and mighty,

The Lord mighty in battle!
Lift up your heads, O ye gates;
Even lift them up, ye everlasting doors;
And the King of glory shall come in.'

"Again, is heard the challenge, 'Who is this King of glory?' For the angels never weary of hearing His name exalted. The escorting angels make reply—

'The Lord of hosts;
He is the King of glory.' Psalm 24:7-10.

"Then the portals of the city of God are opened wide, and the angelic throng sweep through the gates amid a burst of rapturous music" (*The Desire of Ages*, 833).

Jesus' request

"When the great sacrifice had been consummated, Christ ascended on high, refusing the adoration of angels until He had presented the request: 'I will that they also, whom Thou hast given Me, be with Me where I am.' John 17:24. Then with inexpressible love and power came forth the answer from the Father's throne: 'Let all the angels of God worship Him.' Hebrews 1:6. . . . His sacrifice completed, there was given unto Him a name that is above every name" (*The Great Controversy*, 501, 502).

The angels worship Jesus

"The Father's arms encircle His Son, and the word is given. 'Let all the angels of God worship Him.' Hebrews 1:6.
". . . The angel host prostrate themselves before Him, while the glad shout fills all the courts of heaven, 'Worthy is the lamb that was slain to receive power, and riches, and wisdom, and strength, and honor, and glory, and blessing.' Revelation 5:12" (*The Desire of Ages*, 834).

United with Jesus

"The family of heaven and the family of earth are one. For us our Lord ascended, and for us He lives. 'Wherefore He is able also to save them to the uttermost that come unto God by Him, seeing He ever liveth to make intercession for them.' Hebrews 7:2" (*The Desire of Ages*, 835).

Jesus' Gift of the Holy Spirit

John 14:16, 17	Jesus promised His disciples that although He was going to leave them, He would send them the Holy Spirit.
Romans 8:26	"The [Holy] Spirit . . . helps in our weaknesses. . . . We do not know what we should pray for . . . , but the Spirit . . . makes intercession for us."
John 15:26	The Holy Spirit is the Spirit of truth and testifies of Jesus.
John 14:26	Jesus calls the Holy Spirit "the Helper," which means "one called to the side of." He is "called to our side" to encourage, strengthen, convict, teach, and empower us.
John 16:8	When the Holy Spirit comes, He will convict the world of sin.
John 16:13	The Spirit of truth guides us into all truth and, through the prophetic word, reveals the future.
Acts 1:8	The Holy Spirit empowers our witness and makes it effective.
Luke 11:13	God is more willing to give His Holy Spirit to those who ask Him than we are to give good gifts to our children.
James 4:2	Jesus invites us to ask for the Holy Spirit. Asking God for the Holy Spirit prepares our hearts to receive this precious gift.
Zechariah 10:1	We are told to "ask the LORD for rain in the time of the latter rain."
Acts 3:19	There are several prerequisites to receiving the Holy Spirit. Repentance is one of them.

John 14:15, 16	Obedience is another one of Heaven's conditions to receive the Holy Spirit. Jesus linked the keeping of His commandments and the reception of the Holy Spirit.
Hosea 10:12	We can expect the outpouring and infilling of the Holy Spirit as we seek God and by His power live righteously.
Romans 13:11	Now is the time to wake up from spiritual sleep, "for . . . our salvation is nearer than when we first believed."
John 14:17	The world cannot receive the Spirit of truth "because it neither sees Him nor knows Him," but we know Him, for He dwells with us and will be in us.
Revelation 18:1	The earth will be illuminated with the glory of God. This will be accomplished through the outpouring of the Holy Spirit in the closing work of the gospel.
Matthew 24:14	The gospel "will be preached in all the world as a witness to all the nations, and then the end will come."
Revelation 18:4, 5	Jesus makes an appeal to the world under the final outpouring of the Holy Spirit to come out of Babylon. John heard a voice from heaven saying, "Come out of her, my people, lest you share in her sins, and lest you receive of her plagues. For her sins have reached to heaven."
Revelation 3:20	Jesus seeks to enter into every person's heart through the Holy Spirit. He said, "I stand at the door and knock. If anyone hears My voice and opens the door, I will come in to him and dine with him, and he with Me."

FOR FURTHER STUDY

The Holy Spirit is a divine Being

"There are three living persons of the heavenly trio; in the name of these three great powers—the Father, the Son, and the Holy Spirit—those who receive Christ by living faith are baptized, and these powers will co-operate with obedient subjects of heaven in their efforts to live the new life in Christ" (*Evangelism*, 615).

The Holy Spirit is Jesus' representative

"The Holy Spirit is Christ's representative, but divested of the personality of humanity, and independent thereof. Cumbered with humanity, Christ could not be in every place personally. Therefore, it was for their interest that He should go to the Father, and send the Spirit to be His successor on earth. No one could then have any advantage because of his location or his personal contact with Christ. By the Spirit the Saviour would be accessible to all. In this sense He would be nearer to them than if He had not ascended on high" (*The Desire of Ages*, 669).

Our greatest need

"A revival of true godliness among us is the greatest and most urgent of all our needs. To seek this should be our first work. . . . Our heavenly Father is more willing to give His Holy Spirit to them that ask Him, than are earthly parents to give good gifts to their children. But it is our work, by confession, humiliation, repentance, and earnest prayer, to fulfill the conditions upon which God has promised to grant us His blessing. A revival need be expected only in answer to prayer" (*Selected Messages*, book 1, 121).

The latter rain will be more abundant than the former rain

"Ask in faith for the promised blessing, and it will come. The outpouring of the Spirit in the days of the apostles was the 'former rain,' and glorious was the result. But the latter rain will be more abundant" (*Signs of the Times*, February 17, 1914, 3).

The Spirit wants our cooperation

"It is through the sanctification of the spirit and the belief of the truth, that we become laborers together with God. God waits for the co-operation of His church. . . . The object of all this provision of heaven is before us,—the souls for whom Christ died,— and it depends upon us to lay hold of the promises God has given, and become laborers together with him; for divine and human agencies must co-operate in this work" (*Christian Education*, 87).

"There is great need of the Holy Spirit's influence in our midst. There must be an individual work done in the breaking of stubborn hearts. There needs to be deep heart-searching, that will lead to confession of sin" (*Reflecting Christ*, 102).

The outpouring of the Holy Spirit

"The descent of the Holy Spirit upon the church is looked forward to as in the future; but it is the privilege of the church to have it now. Seek for it, pray for it, believe for it. We must have it, and Heaven is waiting to bestow it" (*Advent Review and Sabbath Herald*, March 19, 1895, 2).

"It is not because of any restriction on the part of God that the riches of His grace do not flow earthward to men. If the fulfillment of the promise is not seen as it might be, it is because the promise is not appreciated as it should be. If all were willing, all would be filled with the Spirit" (*The Acts of the Apostles*, 50).

"Near the close of earth's harvest, a special bestowal of spiritual grace is promised to prepare the church for the coming of the Son of man" (*The Acts of the Apostles*, 55).

Influenced by the press

"In a large degree through our publishing houses is to be accomplished the work of that other angel [Revelation 18:1] who comes down from heaven with great power and who lightens the earth with His glory.

"Solemn is the responsibility that rests upon our houses of publi-cation" (*Testimonies for the Church*, vol. 7, 140).

"God will soon do great things for us, if we lie humble and believing at His feet. . . . More than one thousand will soon be converted in one day, most of whom will trace their first convictions to the reading of our publications" (*Advent Review and Sabbath Herald*, November 10, 1885, 12).

The gospel soon to be proclaimed worldwide

"By giving the gospel to the world it is in our power to hasten our Lord's return" (*The Desire of Ages*, 633).

"Advance; enter new territory; lift the standard in every land. 'Arise, shine; for thy light is come, and the glory of the Lord is risen upon thee' " (*Evangelism*, 707).

"The work is soon to close. The members of the church militant who have proved faithful will become the church triumphant" (Letter 32, 1892).

"God will move upon men in humble positions to declare the message of present truth. Many such will be seen hastening hither and thither, constrained by the Spirit of God to give the light to those in darkness. The truth is as a fire in their bones, filling them with a burning desire to enlighten those who sit in darkness. Many, even among the uneducated, will proclaim the word of the Lord. Children will be impelled by the Holy Spirit to go forth to declare the message of heaven. The Spirit will be poured out upon those who yield to His promptings" (*Testimonies for the Church*, vol. 7, 26, 27).

"Multitudes will receive the faith and join the armies of the Lord" (*Advent Review and Sabbath Herald*, July 23, 1895).

"Servants of God, with their faces lighted up and shining with holy consecration, will hasten from place to place to proclaim the message from heaven. By thousands of voices, all over the earth, the warning will be given. Miracles will be wrought, the sick will be healed, and signs and wonders will follow the believers" (*The Great Controversy*, 612).

"The Spirit is given as a regenerating agency, to make effectual the salvation wrought by the death of our Redeemer. The Spirit is constantly seeking to draw the attention of men to the great offering that was made on the cross of Calvary, to unfold to the world the love of God, and to open to the convicted soul the precious things of the Scriptures" (*The Acts of the Apostles*, 52).

18
Jesus Gives Gifts to His Church

Ephesians 4:8   When Jesus ascended to heaven, He imparted spiritual gifts to His church.

1 Corinthians 12:4   The Holy Spirit gives different gifts, ministries, and activities to the people of God.

1 Corinthians 12:7–10   Spiritual gifts are given to build up the body of Christ and empower the church's witness to the world.

1 Corinthians 12:11   The Holy Spirit gives gifts to each believer individually.

1 Corinthians 12:28–31; Ephesians 4:11   Sometimes Jesus calls people to a specific role, such as prophet, pastor, evangelist, teacher, or administrator. At other times, He imparts special abilities, such as organization, teaching, or hospitality, to enable individuals to accomplish their ministry within the church and in the community.

Ephesians 4:12–14   The purpose of these varied gifts is to equip members for their ministry work and to strengthen Christ's church. The gifts are to unify God's people in the faith and knowledge of the Son of God.

Ephesians 4:14   The gifts of the Holy Spirit protect the church from the various winds of false doctrine.

Gifts given to God's church

The gift of speech

John 7:46   No man ever spoke like Jesus.

Matthew 12:34, 35   Jesus spoke in parables to help people understand.

The gift of time

Romans 13:11, 12 Now is the time to live wisely because "our salvation is nearer than when we first believed." So be aware of the times we are living in; stay alert.

Psalm 90:10, 12 Time is short. We are given seventy or eighty years, so we must number our days.

John 17:4 Jesus had enough time to do what the Father commissioned Him to accomplish. He said to His Father, "I have finished the work which You have given Me to do."

The gift of health

3 John 2 "I pray that you may prosper in all things and be in health, just as your soul prospers."

John 10:10 Jesus wants us to be healthy. He said, "I have come that they may have life, and that they may have it more abundantly."

Deuteronomy 4:40 God promised that when we keep His laws and commandments, our lives will be prolonged.

The gift of money

Deuteronomy 8:18 God is the One who gives us the power to get wealth.

John 6:12, 13 Jesus was economical. He did not waste anything. He said to His disciples, "Gather up the fragments that remain, so that nothing is lost."

The gift of love

1 Corinthians 13:13 Paul says the greatest gift of all is love. "Now abide faith, hope, love, these three; but the greatest of these is love."

Gifts remain in the church until Jesus comes

1 Corinthians 1:7, 8 The gifts Jesus gives to His church remain until He comes again.

FOR FURTHER STUDY

The gifts are ours in Christ

"The gifts are already ours in Christ, but their actual possession depends upon our reception of the Spirit of God" (*Christ's Object Lessons*, 327).

"Learning, talents, eloquence, every natural or acquired endowment, may be possessed; but without the presence of the Spirit of God, no heart will be touched, no sinner be won to Christ. On the other hand, if they are connected with Christ, if the gifts of the Spirit are theirs, the poorest and most ignorant of His disciples will have a power that will tell upon hearts" (*Christ's Object Lessons*, 328).

Jesus promises gifts to every believer

"To every person is committed some peculiar gift or talent which is to be used to advance the Redeemer's kingdom" (*Testimonies for the Church*, vol. 4, 618).

"None need lament that they have not received larger gifts; for He who has apportioned to every man is equally honored by the improvement of each trust, whether it be great or small" (*Christ's Object Lessons*, 328).

Using spiritual gifts in ministry

"Every church should be a training school for Christian workers. Its members should be taught how to give Bible readings, how to conduct and teach Sabbath-school classes, how best to help the poor and to care for the sick, how to work for the unconverted. There should be schools of health, cooking schools, and classes in various lines of Christian help work" (*The Ministry of Healing*, 149).

The church is filled with varied gifts

"God's church is the court of holy life, filled with varied gifts and endowed with the Holy Spirit. The members are to find their happiness in the happiness of those whom they help and bless" (*The Acts of the Apostles*, 12).

"Christ's followers have been redeemed for service. Our Lord teaches that the true object of life is ministry. Christ Himself was a worker, and to all His followers He gives the law of service—service to God and to their fellow men. . . . By living to minister for others, man is brought into connection with Christ. The law of service becomes the connecting link which binds us to God and to our fellow men" (*Christ's Object Lessons*, 326).

Gifts given to all

The gift of speech
"The power of speech is a talent that should be diligently cultivated. Of all the gifts we have received from God, none is capable of being a greater blessing than this. With the voice we convince and persuade, with it we offer prayer and praise to God, and with it we tell others of the Redeemer's love. How important, then, that it be so trained as to be most effective for good" (*Christ's Object Lessons*, 335).

"Christ Himself did not suppress one word of truth, but He spoke it always in love. He exercised the greatest tact, and thoughtful, kind attention in His intercourse with the people. He was never rude, never needlessly spoke a severe word, never gave needless pain to a sensitive soul. He did not censure human weakness. He fearlessly denounced hypocrisy, unbelief, and iniquity, but tears were in His voice as He uttered His scathing rebukes" (*The Desire of Ages*, 353).

"Not one word is to be spoken unadvisedly. No evil speaking, no frivolous talk, no fretful repining or impure suggestion, will escape the lips of him who is following Christ. . . .

". . . We should speak of the mercy and loving-kindness of God, of the matchless depths of the Saviour's love. Our words should be words of praise and thanksgiving" (*Christ's Object Lessons*, 337, 338).

The gift of time

"Our time belongs to God. Every moment is His, and we are under the most solemn obligation to improve it to His glory. Of no talent He has given will He require a more strict account than of our time.

"The value of time is beyond computation. Christ regarded every moment as precious, and it is thus that we should regard it. Life is too short to be trifled away. We have but a few days of probation in which to prepare for eternity. We have no time to waste, no time to devote to selfish pleasure, no time for the indulgence of sin" (*Christ's Object Lessons*, 342).

The gift of health

"Pure air, sunlight, abstemiousness, rest, exercise, proper diet, the use of water, trust in divine power—these are the true remedies. Every person should have a knowledge of nature's remedial agencies and how to apply them" (*The Ministry of Healing*, 127).

"The misuse of our physical powers shortens the period of time in which our lives can be used for the glory of God. And it unfits us to accomplish the work God has given us to do. By allowing ourselves to form wrong habits, by keeping late hours, by gratifying appetite at the expense of health, we lay the foundation for feebleness. . . . Those who thus shorten their lives and unfit themselves for service by disregarding nature's laws, are guilty of robbery toward God" (*Christ's Object Lessons*, 346, 347).

The gift of money

"Our money has not been given us that we might honor and glorify ourselves. As faithful stewards we are to use it for the honor and glory of God. . . . All we possess is the Lord's, and we are accountable to Him for the use we make of it. In the use of every penny, it will be seen whether we love God supremely and our neighbor as ourselves" (*Christ's Object Lessons*, 351).

"He who realizes that his money is a talent from God will use it economically, and will feel it a duty to save that he may give" (*Christ's Object Lessons*, 352).

The gift of love

"Love is a precious gift, which we receive from Jesus" (*The Ministry of Healing*, 358).

"Looking unto Jesus we obtain brighter and more distinct views of God, and by beholding we become changed. . . . Growing into His likeness, we enlarge our capacity for knowing God. More and more we enter into fellowship with the heavenly world, and we have continually increasing power to receive the riches of the knowledge and wisdom of eternity" (*Christ's Object Lessons*, 355).

19

Jesus' True Witnesses

Matthew 28:7 Good news is for sharing. The news of the Resurrection was the best news of all, so the angel instructed the women at the tomb to "go quickly" and tell His disciples that He had risen.

Matthew 28:9, 10 When Jesus met the women, His first word was "Rejoice!" The Resurrection is something to rejoice about. He added, "Don't be afraid. Go and tell My brethren to go to Galilee, and there they will see Me."

Mark 16:15 On the hillside in Galilee, the resurrected Christ gave His disciples the Great Commission: "Go into all the world and preach the gospel."

Matthew 28:19, 20 Jesus promised His disciples He would give them the power to complete the task He had given them. The Great Commission was accompanied by the great promise. They were to go and "make disciples of all the nations, baptizing them in the name of the Father and of the Son and of the Holy Spirit, teaching them to observe all things" that He taught them.

Acts 1:8 Jesus promised His disciples that they would receive great power to do a great work.

Colossians 2:15 Jesus defeated the principalities and powers of hell on the cross. In His resurrection, He demonstrated that He has power over the grave. Jesus' commission includes the promise that He has authority over all the forces of evil and will grant His witnessing church the power to defeat the enemy.

Galatians 3:28 The gospel commission has no boundaries. It is for all nations, for all are "one in Christ Jesus."

John 14:15	Accepting the gospel means accepting Christ and His teachings. Jesus appeals to us to be obedient to His commands. He says, "If you love Me, keep My commandments."
Revelation 14:12	God's end-time people are "those who keep the commandments of God and the faith of Jesus."
Matthew 24:14	"This gospel of the kingdom will be preached in all the world as a witness to all the nations, and then the end will come."
Isaiah 52:7	Isaiah gives a description of those who preach the gospel: "How beautiful upon the mountains are the feet of him who brings good news, who proclaims peace."
Acts 2:41, 42, 46, 47	Acts gives the result of the disciples accepting the Great Commission and preaching the gospel. "Those who gladly received his word were baptized; and that day about three thousand souls were added to them [the church]." These newly baptized converts joined the fellowship of believers and became part of Christ's church.
Acts 4:4	The book of Acts is the story of the triumph of the Cross as the disciples preached the Word in the power of the Holy Spirit. "Many of those who heard the word believed; and the number of the men came to be about five thousand."
Acts 6:7	"The word of God spread, and the number of the disciples multiplied greatly in Jerusalem."
Acts 2:4	The disciples communicated the gospel in a large diversity of languages. "And they were all filled with the Holy Spirit and began to speak with other tongues." This gift of "tongues" was the gift of real languages to enable the disciples to preach the gospel in multiple languages they never understood before.

Acts 4:31	They confidently proclaimed the word of God, believing that the power of the Holy Spirit would attend their words and transform lives.
Mark 16:17, 18	In the name of Jesus, the disciples cast out demons, spoke with new tongues (languages), and experienced miracles.
Luke 4:43; 19:10	Christ's prime mission for coming to this world was to share His Father's love and grace by preaching the kingdom of God.
John 9:4	Jesus revealed the importance of working while we have an opportunity. Doors open to the gospel today may close tomorrow. He said, "I must work the works of Him who sent Me while it is day; the night is coming when no one can work."
Proverbs 11:30	The promise for soul winners is sure. "He who wins souls is wise." Placing priority on soul winning is one of life's wisest choices because the results are eternal.
Daniel 12:3	Wise soul winners will shine like the stars forever and ever.

FOR FURTHER STUDY

Jesus' commission to His disciples

"The Saviour's commission to the disciples included all the believers. It includes all believers in Christ to the end of time. It is a fatal mistake to suppose that the work of saving souls depends alone on the ordained minister. . . . All who receive the life of Christ are ordained to work for the salvation of their fellow men. For this work the church was established, and all who take upon themselves its sacred vows are thereby pledged to be co-workers with Christ" (*The Desire of Ages*, 822).

The descent of the Holy Spirit

"The descent of the Holy Spirit upon the church is looked forward to as in the future; but it is the privilege of the church to have it now. Seek for it, pray for it, believe for it. We must have it, and heaven is waiting to bestow it" (*Evangelism*, 701).

Every believer a witness

"Every follower of Jesus has a work to do as a missionary for Christ in the family, in the neighborhood, in the town or city where he lives" (*Testimonies for the Church*, vol. 2, 632).

Faithfulness in fulfilling Jesus' commission

"The very life of the church depends upon her faithfulness in fulfilling the Lord's commission. To neglect this work is surely to invite spiritual feebleness and decay. Where there is no active labor for others, love wanes, and faith grows dim" (*The Desire of Ages*, 825).

Jesus' promise for success

"Christ gave His disciples their commission. He made full provision for the prosecution of the work, and took upon Himself the responsibility for its success. So long as they obeyed His word, and worked in connection with Him, they could not fail. Go to all nations, He bade them. Go to the farthest part of the habitable globe, but know that My presence will be there. Labor in faith and confidence, for the time will never come when I will forsake you" (*The Desire of Ages*, 822).

Proclaiming the gospel to the world

"The disciples began to realize the nature and extent of their work. They were to proclaim to the world the wonderful truths which Christ had entrusted to them. The events of His life, His death and resurrection, the prophecies that pointed to these events, the sacredness of the law of God, the mysteries of the plan of salvation, the power of Jesus for the remission of sins,—to all these things they were witnesses, and they were to make them known to the world. They were to proclaim the gospel of peace and salvation through repentance and the power of the Saviour" (*The Desire of Ages*, 805).

The Great Commission

"Upon us is laid a sacred charge. The commission has been given us: 'Go ye therefore, and make disciples of all nations, baptizing them in the name of the Father, and of the Son, and of the Holy Ghost: teaching them to observe all things whatsoever I have commanded you: and, lo, I am with you alway, even unto the end of the world.' Matthew 28:19, 20, margin" (*Testimonies for the Church*, vol. 9, 20).

Gift of tongues/languages

"The Holy Spirit, assuming the form of tongues of fire, rested upon those assembled. This was an emblem of the gift then bestowed on the disciples, which enabled them to speak with fluency languages with which they had heretofore been unacquainted" (*The Acts of the Apostles*, 39).

"Every known tongue was represented by those assembled. This diversity of languages would have been a great hindrance to the proclamation of the gospel. . . . The Holy Spirit did for them that which they could not have accomplished for themselves in a lifetime. They could now proclaim the truths of the gospel abroad, speaking with accuracy the languages of those for whom they were laboring. This miraculous gift was a strong evidence to the world that their commission bore the signet of heaven. From this time forth the language of the disciples was pure, simple, and accurate, whether they spoke in their native tongue or in a foreign language" (*The Acts of the Apostles*, 39, 40).

Jesus valued each moment

"Throughout His life on earth, Jesus was an earnest and constant worker. He expected much; therefore He attempted much. After He had entered on His ministry, He said, 'I must work the works of Him that sent Me, while it is day: the night cometh, when no man can work.' John 9:4" (*The Desire of Ages*, 73).

"The value of time is beyond computation. Christ regarded every moment as precious, and it is thus that we should regard it. Life is too short to be trifled away. We have but a few days of probation in which to prepare for eternity" (*Christ's Object Lessons*, 342).

The promise of Jesus' presence

"It is in doing Christ's work that the church has the promise of His presence. Go teach all nations, He said; 'and, lo, I am with you alway, even unto the end of the world.' . . . The very life of the church depends upon her faithfulness in fulfilling the Lord's commission. To neglect this work is surely to invite spiritual feebleness and decay. Where there is no active labor for others, love wanes, and faith grows dim" (*The Desire of Ages*, 825).

20
Jesus' Church

Luke 19:10 Jesus' purpose in coming to earth was to "seek and save the lost." His priority was to redeem the human race.

1 Peter 1:18–20 Jesus' life revealed God's loving character, and His death on the cross confirmed His love before the entire universe. As Jesus bore the guilt of our sins, He demonstrated how far divinity would go to save us. We are redeemed by "the precious blood of Christ."

Matthew 26:39, 42, 44 The world trembled in the balance when Jesus cried out three times, Father, not My will, but Your will be done. In Gethsemane, Jesus made the incredibly difficult decision to redeem the human race at any cost to Himself.

Matthew 16:13 Throughout His earthly ministry, Jesus gradually revealed to His disciples His divine mission. In Caesarea Philippi, He asked His disciples a critically important question, "Who do men say that I, the Son of Man, am?"

Matthew 16:14 The disciples answered Jesus, "Some say John the Baptist, some Elijah, and others Jeremiah or one of the prophets."

Matthew 16:15 Jesus asked the disciples, "But who do you say that I am?"

Matthew 16:16 Peter's response was, "You are the Christ, the Son of the living God." It finally dawned upon them that Jesus was divine.

Jesus builds His church

Matthew 16:17–19 Jesus said to Peter, "On this rock [the fact that I am the Son of the living God] I will build My church."

Acts 4:8–11	Peter identified Jesus as the Rock upon which the church is built by quoting a prophecy from Psalm 118:22: "This is the 'stone which was rejected by you builders, which has become the chief cornerstone.' "
Acts 4:12	Peter declared that there is no salvation in anyone except Christ, "for there is no other name under heaven by which we must be saved."
1 Peter 2:4–6	Peter declared we are all "living stones" built upon Christ as the "chief cornerstone" to build a "spiritual house," Christ's church.
1 Corinthians 10:4	Paul spoke of ancient Israel's experience in the wilderness when the people drank from a rock that was the symbol of Christ.
1 Corinthians 3:10, 11	The church is built upon Jesus Christ as its foundation.
Matthew 16:18, 19	Jesus promised that He would build His church and the gates of hell would not prevail against it (see KJV). Then He declared that He would give the keys of the kingdom of heaven to His church. The keys of the kingdom of heaven are the words of Christ and the teachings of Scripture. (See also Luke 11:52.)

The eight major doctrinal teachings of Jesus

Scriptures	Jesus declared, "Sanctify them through by Your truth. Your word is truth" (John 17:17; see also Psalm 119:105; 2 Timothy 3:16; 2 Peter 1:4, 21). In John 8:32, Jesus said, "You shall know the truth, and the truth shall make you free."
Salvation	God loved the world so much He gave His only begotten Son, Jesus, to die for us (John 3:16; see also Acts 4:12; Ephesians 2:8; John 5:39; Romans 5:8–10).

Second Coming	Jesus said, "I go to prepare a place for you. And . . . I will come again and receive you to Myself; that where I am, there you may be also" (John 14:1–3; see also Psalm 50:3; Revelation 1:7; 1 Thessalonians 4:16, 17; Matthew 16:27).
Sabbath	Jesus' custom was to worship each Sabbath (Luke 4:16; see also Genesis 2:1–3; Exodus 20:8–11; John 14:15; Matthew 24:20).
State of the dead	Jesus declared death is a sleep. He said, "Lazarus sleeps, but I go that I may wake him up." Then He stated plainly, "Lazarus is dead" (John 11:11–14; see also Ecclesiastes 9:5; Psalms 115:17; 6:5; 17:15).
Sanctuary/ judgment	Jesus is in heaven's sanctuary interceding for us (Hebrews 7:25; see also Luke 24:50, 51; John 14:1–3; Hebrews 4:12; 12:1, 2).
Standards	Jesus says that if you seek the kingdom of God and His righteousness first, you will be blessed (Matthew 6:33; see also 1 John 2:6, 15–17; Colossians 3:1, 2; Romans 12:1, 2).
Spirit of prophecy	There are two identifying marks of the true church— keeping God's commandments and having the testimony of Jesus (Revelation 12:17). "The testimony of Jesus is the spirit of prophecy" (Revelation 19:10; see also Ephesians 4:8–16; 1 Corinthians 1:4–9; Matthew 7:15–20; 1 John 4:2; 1 Corinthians 12:27, 28).
John 8:12	Jesus said, "I am the light of the world. He who follows Me shall not walk in darkness."
John 14:6	Jesus said, "I am the way, the truth, and the life." Jesus is the way of salvation. He has revealed the truth of His word so that we can have eternal life.

Characteristics of Jesus' church

Revelation 12:17   God's last-day church will keep the commandments of God and have the testimony of Jesus Christ. Revelation 14:12 adds, "Here are those who keep the commandments of God and the faith of Jesus." God's end-time people keep the commandments, including the Sabbath.

Revelation 19:10   The Bible defines the second characteristic listed in Revelation 12:17, the testimony of Jesus, as the spirit of prophecy.

Ephesians 4:8–16   The gift of prophecy will be one of the gifts of the Spirit in Christ's true church at the end time.

Matthew 28:19, 20   God's last-day church is a worldwide movement. Jesus' great commission to His disciples was to go into all the world with the gospel.

FOR FURTHER STUDY

Jesus' glory revealed

"Peter had expressed the faith of the twelve. Yet the disciples were still far from understanding Christ's mission. . . . They did not see their way clearly. . . . From time to time precious rays of light from Jesus shone upon them, yet often they were like men groping among shadows. But on this day, before they were brought face to face with the great trial of their faith, the Holy Spirit rested upon them in power. . . . Beneath the guise of humanity they discerned the glory of the Son of God" (*The Desire of Ages*, 412).

Jesus the Cornerstone

" 'Upon this rock,' said Jesus, 'I will build My church.' In the presence of God, and the heavenly intelligences, in the presence of the unseen army of hell, Christ founded His church upon the living Rock. That

Rock is Himself,—His own body, for us broken and bruised. Against the church built upon this foundation, the gates of hell shall not prevail" (*The Desire of Ages*, 413).

The foundation of faith

"How feeble the church appeared when Christ spoke these words! There was only a handful of believers, against whom all the power of demons and evil men would be directed; yet the followers of Christ were not to fear. Built upon the Rock of their strength, they could not be overthrown. . . .

"Peter had expressed the truth which is the foundation of the church's faith, and Jesus now honored him as the representative of the whole body of believers" (*The Desire of Ages*, 413).

Keys of the kingdom

"He [Jesus] said, 'I will give unto thee the keys of the kingdom of heaven: and whatsoever thou shalt bind on earth shall be bound in heaven: and whatsoever thou shalt loose on earth shall be loosed in heaven.' [Matthew 16:19.]

" 'The keys of the kingdom of heaven' are the words of Christ. All the words of Holy Scripture are His, and are here included. These words have power to open and to shut heaven. They declare the conditions upon which men are received or rejected. Thus, the work of those who preach God's word is a savor of life unto life or of death unto death. Theirs is a mission weighted with eternal results" (*The Desire of Ages*, 413, 414).

Two characteristics of the true church in Revelation 12:17

"Those who keep the commandments of God and have the testimony of Jesus Christ."

The Sabbath

" 'The importance of the Sabbath as the memorial of creation is that it keeps ever present the true reason why worship is due to God'—because He is the Creator, and we are His creatures. 'The Sabbath therefore lies at the very foundation of divine worship, for it teaches this great truth in the most impressive manner, and no other institution does this. The true ground of divine worship, not of that on the seventh day merely, but of all worship, is found in the distinction between the Creator and His creatures. This great fact can never become obsolete, and must never be forgotten.'—J. N. Andrews, *History of the Sabbath*, chapter 27. It was to keep this truth ever before the minds of men, that God instituted the Sabbath in Eden; and so long as the fact that He is our Creator continues to be a reason why we should worship Him, so long the Sabbath will continue as its sign and memorial" (*The Great Controversy*, 437, 438).

The Sabbath a sign of loyalty

"Had the Sabbath been universally kept, man's thoughts and affections would have been led to the Creator as the object of reverence and worship, and there would never have been an idolater, an atheist, or an infidel. The keeping of the Sabbath is a sign of loyalty to the true God. 'Him that made heaven, and earth, and the sea, and fountains of waters.' It follows that the message which commands men to worship God and keep His commandments will especially call upon them to keep the fourth commandment" (*The Great Controversy*, 438).

The gift of prophecy

"The Lord has sent His people much instruction, line upon line, precept upon precept, here a little, and there a little. Little heed is given to the Bible, and the Lord has given a lesser light to lead men and women to the greater light. Oh, how much good would be accomplished if the books containing this light were read with a determination to carry out the principles they contain! There would be a thousandfold greater vigilance, a thousandfold more self-denial and resolute effort. And many more would now be rejoicing in the light of present truth" (*Colporteur Ministry*, 125, 126).

21

Jesus' Sanctuary Message

Revelation 14:6   Jesus' urgent last-day message to the entire world: "Then I saw another angel flying in the midst of heaven, having the everlasting gospel to preach to those who dwell on the earth—to every nation, tribe, tongue, and people."

Revelation 14:7   Heaven's announcement of the judgment hour: "Fear God and give glory to Him, for the hour of His judgment has come; and worship Him who made heaven and earth, the sea and springs of water."

Daniel 12:4   God's promise that knowledge of His prophetic word would increase at the end time: "But you, Daniel, shut up the words, and seal the book until the time of the end; many shall run to and fro, and knowledge shall increase."

Acts 17:31   Jesus has appointed a day when He will judge the world.

Daniel 7:13   In Daniel's vision, the "Son of Man" (Jesus) approaches His Father to participate in the judgment before His return to earth.

Daniel 7:9, 10   In prophetic vision, Daniel watched as "thrones were put in place, and the Ancient of Days [the Father] was seated. . . . Ten thousand times ten thousand stood before Him." The judgment began, "and the books were opened."

Daniel 8:14   "For two thousand three hundred days; then the sanctuary shall be cleansed."

Daniel 8:27   Daniel didn't understand the vision, and he "fainted and was sick for days." The word translated "cleansed" in verse 14 can also be translated as "restored" or "vindicated." The truth about Jesus' heavenly priesthood and the sanctuary would be restored at the end of the 2,300 prophetic days.

Daniel 9:21–23   The angel Gabriel assured Daniel that he would give him "skill to understand" the vision.

What is the sanctuary?

Exodus 25:8   God instructed Moses to make a sanctuary that He might "dwell among them."

Exodus 25:40   The earthly sanctuary was a copy—a miniature model—of the sanctuary in heaven.

Romans 6:23   Since the wages of sin is death, the sinner must bring an animal sacrifice to the court of the sanctuary. (See Leviticus 4 in its entirety.) Once the animal was slain by the sinner and his sins confessed, the priest took the blood into the sanctuary and sprinkled it before the veil separating the Holy from the Most Holy place. The ark of the covenant, containing the Ten Commandments, was in the Most Holy Place behind the veil. The sprinkled blood in the ancient sanctuary represented Christ's atonement for our breaking His divine law.

John 1:29   The lamb that was slain represents Jesus, the Lamb who takes away the sins of the world.

Hebrews 8:5   The earthly sanctuary was a "copy and shadow" of the heavenly sanctuary.

Hebrews 8:1   Jesus, our High Priest, is "at the right hand of the throne of the Majesty in the heavens, a Minister of the sanctuary and of the true tabernacle which the Lord" built.

Cleansing of the sanctuary

Hebrews 9:24   "For Christ has not entered the holy places made with hands, which are copies of the true, but into heaven itself, now to appear in the presence of God for us."

Daniel 7:10   Daniel saw the cleansing of heaven's sanctuary in the last-day judgment. "The court was seated, and the books were opened."

Daniel 8:14	"For two thousand three hundred days; then the sanctuary shall be cleansed." The expression "the cleansing of the sanctuary" has multiple rich meanings. It refers to the pre-Advent judgment before the coming of Jesus. It also speaks of the restoration of the truth about Jesus' ministry in the sanctuary and the law of God. Finally, it speaks of the blotting out of sin from heaven's records on behalf of the righteous and the final vindication and triumph of Jesus and His people.
Ezekiel 4:6	In Bible prophecy, a day represents a year. "I have laid on you a day for each year" (see also Numbers 14:34). As a result, the 2,300 prophetic days equal 2,300 literal years.
Daniel 8:17	The angel Gabriel says to Daniel, "Understand, son of man, that the vision refers to the time of the end."
Daniel 8:19	Gabriel says, "Look, I am making known to you what shall happen in the latter time of the indignation; for at the appointed time the end shall be."
Daniel 9:25	The angel told Daniel the seventy weeks, or 490 years, would begin at the command to restore and build Jerusalem, then added that

> "from the going forth of the command
> To restore and build Jerusalem
> Until Messiah the Prince,
> There shall be seven weeks and sixty-two weeks."

The decree to rebuild Jerusalem and restore worship was proclaimed in the seventh year of Artaxerxes, in 457 BC. Based on the day-for-a-year principle, 483 years from the decree to rebuild and restore Jerusalem is AD 27, the year of the anointing at the baptism of the Messiah.

Jesus the Anointed One

Luke 3:21, 22   Jesus was baptized by John in AD 27. "The Holy Spirit descended in bodily form like a dove upon Him, and a voice came from heaven which said, 'You are My beloved Son; in You I am well pleased.' "

Acts 10:37, 38   At Jesus' baptism, He was anointed by the Holy Spirit. "God anointed Jesus of Nazareth with the Holy Spirit and with power, who went about doing good and healing all who were oppressed by the devil, for God was with Him."

Daniel 9:26   "And after the sixty-two weeks Messiah shall be cut off, but not for Himself." The sacrifice of Christ was for us. It was for us that He suffered, died, and bore the guilt of our sins (see Galatians 3:13; 2 Corinthians 5:21).

Daniel 9:27   In the middle of the last week of the sixty-nine-week prophecy, Jesus, the Messiah, would be crucified, or "cut off." One half of seven, the last week of the seventy-week prophecy, is three and a half years. Three and a half years from the fall of AD 27 takes us to the spring of AD 31, exactly the time of the Passover.

Note: Jesus was baptized in AD 27, crucified in AD 31; the gospel went to the Gentiles in AD 34. The first 490 years of this prophecy have to do with the Jewish nation and the first coming of Christ. If the 490 years run out in AD 34 and there are still 1,810 days (years) left in the 2,300-day prophecy, these remaining days (years) would lead us to AD 1844. In 1844, the pre-Advent judgment began in heaven. At this precise moment, Jesus sent the message of His last-day ministry in heaven's sanctuary and the final proclamation of His eternal truth to the world. This timeline is illustrated in the following chart:

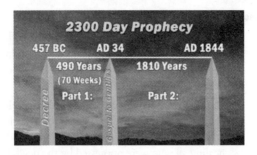

2300 Day Prophecy

457 BC · AD 34 · AD 1844

490 Years (70 Weeks) — 1810 Years

Decree · Gospel to Gentiles

Part 1: · Part 2:

FOR FURTHER STUDY

The pre-Advent judgment

" 'A fiery stream issued and came forth from before Him: thousand thousands ministered unto Him, and ten thousand times ten thousand stood before Him: the judgment was set, and the books were opened.' Daniel 7:9, 10.

"Thus was presented to the prophet's vision the great and solemn day when the characters and the lives of men should pass in review before the Judge of all the earth, and to every man should be rendered 'according to his works.' The Ancient of Days is God the Father. . . . And holy angels as ministers and witnesses, in number 'ten thousand times ten thousand, and thousands of thousands,' attend this great tribunal" (*The Great Controversy*, 479).

"The coming of Christ here described is not His second coming to the earth. He comes to the Ancient of Days in heaven to receive dominion and glory and a kingdom, which will be given Him at the close of His work as a mediator. . . . Attended by heavenly angels, our great High Priest enters the holy of holies and there appears in the presence of God to engage in the last acts of His ministration in behalf of man—to perform the work of investigative judgment and to make an atonement for all who are shown to be entitled to its benefits" (*The Great Controversy*, 480).

"So in the great day of final atonement and investigative judgment the only cases considered are those of the professed people of God. The judgment of the wicked is a distinct and separate work, and takes place at a later period" (*The Great Controversy*, 480).

The heavenly sanctuary

"The 'true tabernacle' in heaven is the sanctuary of the new covenant. . . . At the termination of the 2300 days, in 1844, there had been no sanctuary on earth for many centuries. Thus, the prophecy, 'Unto two thousand and three hundred days; then shall the sanctuary be cleansed,' unquestionably points to the sanctuary in heaven" (*The Great Controversy*, 417).

The 2,300 days explained

"The 2300 days had been found to begin when the commandment of Artaxerxes for the restoration and building of Jerusalem went into effect, in the autumn of 457 B.C. Taking this as the starting point, there was perfect harmony in the application of all the events foretold in the explanation of that period in Daniel 9:25-27. Sixty-nine weeks, the first 483 of the 2300 years, were to reach to the Messiah, the Anointed One; and Christ's baptism and anointing by the Holy Spirit, A.D. 27, exactly fulfilled the specification. In the midst of the seventieth week, Messiah was to be cut off. Three and a half years after His baptism, Christ was crucified, in the spring of A.D. 31. The seventy weeks, or 490 years, were to pertain especially to the Jews. At the expiration of this period the nation sealed its rejection of Christ by the persecution of His disciples, and the apostles turned to the Gentiles, A.D. 34. The first 490 years of the 2300 having then ended, 1810 years would remain. From A.D. 34, 1810 years extend to 1844. 'Then,' said the angel, 'shall the sanctuary be cleansed.' All the preceding specifications of the prophecy had been unquestionably fulfilled at the time appointed" (*The Great Controversy*, 410).

God's leading in the Advent movement

"God had led His people in the great advent movement; His power and glory had attended the work, and He would not permit it to end in darkness and disappointment, to be reproached as a false and fanatical excitement. He would not leave His word involved in doubt and uncertainty. Though many abandoned their former reckoning of the prophetic periods and denied the correctness of the movement based thereon, others were unwilling to renounce points of faith and experience that were sustained by the Scriptures and by the witness of the Spirit of God. They believed that they had adopted sound principles of interpretation in their study of the prophecies, and that it was their duty to hold fast the truths already gained, and to continue the same course of Biblical research. With earnest prayer they reviewed their position and studied the Scriptures to discover their mistake. As they could see no error in their reckoning of the prophetic periods, they were led to examine more closely the subject of the sanctuary.

"In their investigation they learned that there is no Scripture evidence sustaining the popular view that the earth is the sanctuary; but they found in the Bible a full explanation of the subject of the sanctuary, its nature, location, and services; the testimony of the sacred writers being so clear and ample as to place the matter beyond all question" (*The Great Controversy*, 410, 411).

22

Jesus, Our High Priest

Matthew 27:50, 51   When Jesus died, He shouted, "It is finished," (see John 19:30) and the veil of the temple was torn in two from top to bottom. This signified that the priestly services of the earthly sanctuary were finished.

Revelation 5:6   Jesus appears in heaven as the slain Lamb interceding at God's throne for us.

Hebrews 7:25   Jesus, our High Priest, is pleading for us. "He is also able to save to the uttermost those who come to God through Him, since He always lives to make intercession for us."

1 Timothy 2:5   Jesus is our Mediator. "For there is one God and one Mediator between God and men, the Man Christ Jesus."

Hebrews 8:3   Paul describes Jesus' ministry as High Priest: "For every high priest is ordained to offer both gifts and sacrifices. Therefore it is necessary that this One [Jesus] also have something to offer."

Hebrews 5:1   Jesus acts for us in the sanctuary. "Every high priest taken from among men is ordained for men in things pertaining to God, that he may offer both gifts and sacrifices for sins" (KJV).

Review of Adventist history

Daniel 8:14   Early Adventists studied the book of Daniel and the 2,300-year prophecy. "For two thousand three hundred days; then the sanctuary shall be cleansed." They believed that the cleansing of the sanctuary was the cleansing of the earth by fire.

Revelation 10:9, 10	Since Jesus did not return as they expected on October 22, 1844, the Adventists were deeply disappointed. This understanding was "sweet as honey" in their mouths, but when they had "eaten" it, their stomachs became bitter.
Revelation 10:11	They "must prophesy again about many peoples, nations, tongues, and kings."

Christ's high-priestly work of judgment

Leviticus 16:4	To understand Christ's priestly work, it is essential to understand the priest's work in the Old Testament on the Day of Atonement. On the Day of Atonement, the high priest had to bathe and put on the holy garments of white linen, followed by a linen sash and the white linen turban.
Hebrews 9:24	Jesus appears in the presence of God for us.
Hebrews 9:22	"Without shedding of blood there is no remission" of sins.
Acts 3:19–21	We need to confess and repent of our sins so that God will blot out our sins and refresh our souls by giving us the Holy Spirit, whom Jesus has promised to all who accept Him.
1 Peter 4:17	Judgment begins at the house of God. "If it begins with us first, what will be the end of those who do not obey the gospel of God?"
Leviticus 16:21	On the Day of Atonement, Aaron, the high priest, laid his hands on the head of the live goat and confessed "all the iniquities of the children of Israel, . . . putting them on the head of the goat," which he sent "away into the wilderness."
Hebrews 10:10	It is because Jesus did His Father's will and offered His own body that we are cleansed from sin and accepted as holy.

Leviticus 23:27, 29	Anyone who was not "afflicted" on the Day of Atonement would be "cut off," no longer part of the chosen people.
Ephesians 2:12	They would become, in effect, Gentiles, "aliens from the commonwealth of Israel and strangers from the covenants of promise, having no hope and without God in the world."
2 Corinthians 5:10	We will all be judged by Jesus Christ, and He will hold us accountable for what we have done, whether it was good or bad.
Daniel 7:22	The Ancient of Days (the Father) decides in favor of God's people and announces that the time has come for them to have their own kingdom.
Ecclesiastes 12:13, 14	"God will bring every work into judgment, including every secret thing, whether good or evil."
1 Corinthians 4:5	Don't judge others before God's judgment comes. God will decide. Everything will be made plain, and He will bring all things to light, including our motives.
Hebrews 4:14–16	We have a wonderful High Priest, Jesus Christ. He sympathizes with us because He was tempted in all points without sinning. We can "therefore come boldly to the throne of grace, that we may obtain mercy and find grace to help in time of need."
Hebrews 9:24	We have an intercessor, Jesus Christ, who appears before the Father on our behalf.
Hebrews 6:17	God showed us His intention to keep His promise so we could understand. He confirmed His promise to Abraham by an oath.
Hebrews 6:18	God's promise rests on two unchangeable facts: one fact is that God never lies, and the other is that He confirmed what He said by an oath. Therefore, we can hold to this hope with absolute assurance. This is what gives us courage.

Hebrews 6:19	This hope is an anchor for our souls. Our hope is not in ourselves; it is in Jesus Christ, our Intercessor.
Hebrews 6:20	Jesus serves as our High Priest after the eternal priestly order of Melchizedek.
Revelation 22:11	When Christ finishes His priestly work in the heavenly sanctuary before His return, those who are unjust will continue to be unjust, and those who are filthy will remain filthy. The righteous will continue to be righteous, and the holy remain holy.

FOR FURTHER STUDY

The foundation of our faith

"The correct understanding of the ministration in the heavenly sanctuary is the foundation of our faith. . . .

". . . The subject of the sanctuary and the investigative judgment should be clearly understood by the people of God. All need a knowledge for themselves of the position and work of their great High Priest" (*Evangelism*, 221, 222).

Prophetic periods

"The preaching of a definite time for the judgment, in the giving of the first message, was ordered of God. The computation of the prophetic periods on which that message was based, placing the close of the 2300 days in the autumn of 1844, stands without impeachment" (*The Great Controversy*, 457).

"The subject of the sanctuary was the key which unlocked the mystery of the disappointment of 1844. It opened to view a complete system of truth, connected and harmonious, showing that God's hand had directed the great advent movement and revealing present duty as it brought to light the position and work of His people" (*The Great Controversy*, 423).

The judgment hour

"The announcement, 'The hour of His judgment is come,' points to the closing work of Christ's ministration for the salvation of men. It heralds a truth which must be proclaimed until the Saviour's intercession shall cease and He shall return to the earth to take His people to Himself. The work of judgment which began in 1844 must continue until the cases of all are decided, both living and the dead; hence it will extend to the close of human probation. That men may be prepared to stand in the judgment, the message commands them to 'fear God, and give glory to Him' 'and worship Him that made heaven, and earth, and the sea, and the fountains of waters.' The result of an acceptance of the messages is given in the word: 'Here are they that keep the commandments of God, and the faith of Jesus.' In order to be prepared for the judgment, it is necessary that men should keep the law of God" (*The Great Controversy*, 435, 436).

Final atonement and investigative judgment

"In the typical service only those who had come before God with confession and repentance, and whose sins, through the blood of the sin offering, were transferred to the sanctuary, had a part in the service of the Day of Atonement. So in the great day of final atonement and investigative judgment the only cases considered are those of the professed people of God. The judgment of the wicked is a distinct and separate work, and takes place at a later period. 'Judgment must begin at the house of God: and if it first begins at us, what shall the end be of them that obey not the gospel?' 1 Peter 4:17" (*The Great Controversy*, 480).

Jesus our High Priest and Intercessor

"All who have truly repented of sin, and by faith claimed the blood of Christ as their atoning sacrifice, have had pardon entered against their names in the books of heaven; as they have become partakers of the righteousness of Christ, and their characters are found to be in harmony with the law of God, their sins will be blotted out, and they themselves will be accounted worthy of eternal life" (*Christ in His Sanctuary*, 177, 178).

Every deed brought into judgment

"In the judgment the use made of every talent will be scrutinized. How have we employed the capital lent us of Heaven? Will the Lord at His coming receive His own with usury? Have we improved the powers entrusted us, in hand and heart and brain, to the glory of God and the blessing of the world? How have we used our time, our pen, our voice, our money, our influence? What have we done for Christ, in the person of the poor, the afflicted, the orphan, or the widow?" (*The Great Controversy*, 487).

Jesus our Intercessor

"As our Intercessor, His office work is to introduce us to God as His sons and daughters. Christ intercedes in behalf of those who have received Him. To them He gives power, by virtue of His own merits, to become members of the royal family, children of the heavenly King. And the Father demonstrates His infinite love for Christ, who paid our ransom with His blood, by receiving and welcoming Christ's friends as His friends. He is satisfied with the atonement made. He is glorified by the incarnation, the life, death, and mediation of His Son.

"As Christ intercedes in our behalf, the Father lays open all the treasures of His grace for our appropriation, to be enjoyed and to be communicated to others" (*Testimonies for the Church*, vol. 6, 363, 364).

23

Jesus' Signs of His Second Coming

John 14:3 — Just before His death, resurrection, and ascension into heaven, Jesus promised His disciples He would return one day to take them home.

Matthew 23:38, 39 — Jesus told the Jewish leaders that they would not see Him again until they would say, "Blessed is He who comes in the Name of the Lord."

Matthew 24:1–44 — Jesus outlined the signs that would precede His coming and the end of the age.

Matthew 24:2 — Jesus told His disciples that not one stone of the temple would be left on another.

Matthew 24:3 — When Jesus told His disciples that not one stone would be left upon another in the temple, they thought He was talking about the final destruction at the end of the world, so they asked, "What will be the sign of Your coming, and of the end of the age?"

Celestial signs

Matthew 24:29 — Jesus told His disciples that after the tribulation, "the sun will be darkened, the moon will not give its light; the stars will fall from heaven, and the powers of the heavens will be shaken." These signs would take place when the Dark Ages were coming to an end and in this precise order, a dark day, the moon not giving its light, and the falling of the stars.

Signs in the religious world

Matthew 24:5 — Jesus said, "Many will come in My name, saying, 'I am the Christ,' and will deceive many."

Matthew 24:23	Jesus said, "If anyone says to you, 'Look, here is the Christ!' or 'There!' do not believe it."
Matthew 24:24	Jesus said, "False christs and false prophets will arise and show great signs and wonders to deceive, if possible, even the elect."

Signs in the political world

Matthew 24:6	Jesus said, "You will hear of wars and rumors of wars. See that you are not troubled; for all these things must come to pass, but the end is not yet."
Luke 21:26	Jesus declared that "men's hearts [would be] failing them from fear and the expectation of those things which are coming on the earth, for the powers of the heavens will be shaken."
Revelation 11:18	Christ will return and "destroy those who destroy the earth." Now, for the first time in history, the human race has the capacity for self-destruction by using nuclear warheads.

Signs in the natural world

Matthew 24:7	Jesus said, "Nation will rise against nation, and kingdom against kingdom. And there will be famines, pestilences, and earthquakes in various places."

Signs in the social world

Matthew 24:12	Jesus said in the last days, "lawlessness will abound, [and] the love of many will grow cold."

Signs in the economic world

James 5:1–6	The Scriptures predict that in the last days, there will be a sudden economic collapse because those living in the world have heaped up treasures for themselves. The world has lived in pleasure and luxury.

Gospel to the world—the last sign of Jesus' return

Matthew 24:14 Jesus said, "This gospel of the kingdom will be preached in all the world as a witness to all the nations, and then the end will come."

The exact time not revealed

Mark 13:29 Jesus has not revealed the exact time of His coming, but He said, "When you see these things happening, know that it is near—at the very doors!"

Luke 21:36 Jesus says to watch, keep awake, and pray. Be ready!

Matthew 24:30 Jesus' glorious promise is that one day He will return in glory. "Then the sign of the Son of Man will appear in heaven, and then all the tribes of the earth will mourn, and they will see the Son of Man coming on the clouds of heaven with power and great glory."

FOR FURTHER STUDY

Jesus went from the signs of the destruction of Jerusalem to the signs in the end times

"He [Jesus] mingled the description of these two events. Had He opened to His disciples future events as He beheld them, they would have been unable to endure the sight. In mercy to them He blended the description of the two great crises, leaving the disciples to study out the meaning for themselves" (*The Desire of Ages*, 628).

"From the destruction of Jerusalem, Christ passed on rapidly to the greater event, the last link in the chain of this earth's history,—the coming of the Son of God in majesty and glory. Between these two events, there lay open to Christ's view long centuries of darkness, centuries for His church marked with blood and tears and agony. Upon these scenes His disciples could not then endure to look, and Jesus passed them by with a brief mention" (*The Desire of Ages*, 630, 631).

Celestial signs

"At the close of the great papal persecution, Christ declared, the sun should be darkened, and the moon should not give her light. Next, the stars should fall from heaven" (*The Desire of Ages*, 632).

"This was the first of the signs in the heavens ordained to herald the imminence of our Lord's return" (*The Seventh-day Adventist Bible Commentary*, vol. 5, 502).

Evidence
Fulfilled with the Dark Day of May 19, 1780—The sun was darkened, and the moon's light was veiled.

Fulfilled on November 13, 1833—Shooting stars were seen in the skies in unprecedented numbers.

Signs in the religious world

"As one of the signs of Jerusalem's destruction, Christ had said, 'Many false prophets shall rise, and shall deceive many.' False prophets did rise, deceiving the people, and leading great numbers into the desert. . . . But this prophecy was spoken also for the last days. This sign is given as a sign of the second advent. Even now false christs and false prophets are showing signs and wonders to seduce His disciples" (*The Desire of Ages*, 631).

Evidence
Spiritualism, psychic practices, religious cults, and cult leaders are rising rapidly, with hundreds of thousands of cult followers worldwide. These cults often have a charismatic leader who claims divinity.

Evidence
It is estimated that 5 million to 7 million Americans have been involved in cults or cultlike groups.

Signs in the political world

"The judgments of God are in the land. The wars and rumors of wars, the destruction by fire and flood, say clearly that the time of trouble, which is to increase until the end, is very near at hand. We have no time to lose. The world is stirred with the spirit of war" (*Advent Review and Sabbath Herald*, November 24, 1904, 16).

Evidence
Approximately 180 million people died in wars during the twentieth century. Here is a partial list of conflicts in the twentieth and the first part of the twenty-first century.

- World War I
- World War II
- Vietnam War
- Korean War
- Sino-Indian War
- Iran-Iraq War
- Afghanistan War
- Persian Gulf War
- Iraq War
- Tribal conflicts in Africa
- Acts of terrorism—a new kind of war

Signs in the natural world

"The time is at hand when there will be sorrow in the world that no human balm can heal. The Spirit of God is being withdrawn. Disasters by sea and by land follow one another in quick succession. How frequently we hear of earthquakes and tornadoes, of destruction by fire and flood, with great loss of life and property! Apparently, these calamities are capricious outbreaks of disorganized, unregulated forces of nature, wholly beyond the control of man; but in them all, God's purpose may be read. They are among the agencies by which He seeks to arouse men and women to a sense of their danger" (*Prophets and Kings*, 277).

Evidence

1. *Famines.* Ten thousand people a day, or more than 3.5 million per year, die of starvation. There are food shortages in at least forty countries.

2. *Earthquakes.* In the past hundred years alone, we have had 1.5 million earthquakes.

3. *Pestilences.* A pestilence refers to a widespread disease that affects human beings, animals, or crops. The health problems with pesticides are becoming well-known. Toxic pollutants poured into the air are causing even more deaths. Such strange diseases as COVID-19, SARS, AIDS, the Marburg virus, Lyme disease, and a host of others are evidence Jesus' prediction is being fulfilled.

4. *Tsunamis.* Major tsunamis have increased around the world. The Asian tsunami disaster on December 26, 2004, killed over 200,000 people instantly.

5. *Hurricanes.* In 2020, the Atlantic hurricane season had the most named storms in history. The 2005 storm Hurricane Katrina was the costliest storm ever recorded in history, with over $75 billion in damage. In 2018 there were 15 named storms with billions of dollars in damages. Tornadoes and cyclones are also on the rise, taking their toll on thousands of lives and causing billions in property damage.

Signs in the social world

"Many fix their eyes upon the terrible wickedness existing around them, the apostasy and weakness on every side, and they talk of these things until their hearts are filled with sadness and doubt. They keep uppermost before the mind the masterly working of the archdeceiver and dwell upon the discouraging features of their experience, while they seem to lose sight of the heavenly Father's power and His matchless love. . . . We must talk of the mightiness of Christ. . . . The Son of the Highest has strength to fight the battle for us, and 'through Him that loved us' we may come off 'more than conquerors' " (*Testimonies for the Church*, vol. 5, 741).

Evidence

In many of the world's major cities, the streets are unsafe. Violent crime is increasing worldwide.

Signs in the economic world

"But there are not many, even among educators and statesmen, who comprehend the causes that underlie the present state of society. Those who hold the reins of government are unable to solve the problem of poverty, pauperism, and increasing crime. They are struggling in vain to place business operations on a more secure basis" (*The Ministry of Healing*, 183).

Evidence

The entire global economy is on shaky ground. America's national debt is enormous at 27 trillion dollars. Trusted financial institutions have collapsed. Thousands have lost their homes and jobs. Nations are facing bankruptcy. The international economy is stretched beyond its capacity to supply society's demands. These unstable economic conditions are another sign of the coming of the Lord.

Gospel to the world—the last sign of Jesus' return

"The heavenly gates are again to be lifted up, and with ten thousand times ten thousand and thousands of thousands of holy ones, our Saviour will come forth as King of kings and Lord of lords. . . .

"But before that coming, Jesus said, 'This gospel of the kingdom shall be preached in all the world for a witness unto all nations.' Matthew 24:14. His kingdom will not come until the good tidings of His grace have been carried to all the earth. Hence, as we give ourselves to God, and win other souls to Him, we hasten the coming of His kingdom" (*Thoughts From the Mount of Blessing*, 108, 109).

"By giving the gospel to the world it is in our power to hasten our Lord's return. We are not only to look for but to hasten the coming of the day of God. 2 Peter 3:12, margin. Had the church of Christ done her appointed work as the Lord ordained, the whole world would before this have been warned, and the Lord Jesus would have come to our earth in power and great glory" (*The Desire of Ages*, 633, 634).

Evidence
The gospel is being proclaimed to the ends of the earth today through television, radio, the internet, the printed page, and personal and public witness. The Holy Spirit is moving powerfully to lead thousands into God's church today. Seventh-day Adventism is one of the fastest-growing Protestant denominations, with over a million people being baptized into membership each year and more than 22 million members in over two hundred countries.

The exact time not revealed

"There are those who claim to know the very day and hour of our Lord's appearing. Very earnest are they in mapping out the future. But the Lord has warned them off the ground they occupy. The exact time of the second coming of the Son of man is God's mystery" (*The Desire of Ages*, 632, 633).

"Soon there appears in the east a small black cloud, about half the size of a man's hand. It is the cloud which surrounds the Saviour, and which seems in the distance to be shrouded in darkness. The people of God know this to be the sign of the Son of man. In solemn silence they gaze upon it as it draws nearer the earth, becoming lighter and more glorious, until it is a great white cloud, its base a glory like consuming fire, and above it the rainbow of the covenant" (*The Great Controversy*, 640, 641).

24
The Manner of Jesus' Second Coming

Titus 2:13
Christians down through the ages have anticipated "the blessed hope and glorious appearing of our great God and Savior Jesus Christ."

John 14:1–3
Jesus reassured His disciples with these words: "Let not your heart be troubled; you believe in God, believe also in Me. . . . I go to prepare a place for you. And if I go and prepare a place for you, I will come again and receive you to Myself; that where I am, there you may be also."

Mark 13:26
Jesus promised that when He returned, we would see Him "coming in the clouds with great power and glory."

Mark 13:27
When Jesus returns, "He will send His angels, and gather together His elect from the four winds, from the farthest part of the earth."

Acts 1:9–11
As the disciples gazed up into heaven, watching in amazement as Christ ascended, His angelic hosts informed them that Jesus would return just as He ascended, literally in the clouds of heaven.

Revelation 1:7
When Jesus comes, "every eye will see Him, even they who pierced Him."

Matthew 24:30
Jesus' return is not a secret event. The saved and the unsaved will see Him coming gloriously in the clouds of heaven.

1 Thessalonians 4:16
Jesus' second coming will be an audible event. He "will descend from heaven with a shout, with the voice of an archangel, and with the trumpet of God."

Psalm 50:3, 4 When Christ returns, every inhabitant of the earth will know it. He will "not keep silent."

Matthew 16:27 Jesus' coming will be a glorious event. He "will come in the glory of His Father with His angels."

Revelation 16:17 Jesus' second coming will be a climactic event. When He comes, "a loud voice [proceeds] out of the temple of heaven, from the throne, saying, 'It is done!' "

Revelation 16:18 "There were great noises, and lightnings; and . . . a great earthquake, such a mighty and great earthquake as had not occurred since men were on the earth."

Revelation 6:15, 16 There is a fearful reaction of the wicked when Jesus comes the second time. "The kings of the earth, the great men, the rich men, the commanders, the mighty men, every slave and every free man, hid themselves in the caves and in the rocks of the mountains, and said to the mountains and rocks, 'Fall on us and hide us from the face of Him who sits on His throne and from the wrath of Lamb!' "

2 Thessalonians 1:9 The wicked who are alive when Jesus comes again will be "punished with everlasting destruction from the presence of the Lord and from the glory of His power."

1 Thessalonians 4:16, 17 "The dead in Christ will rise first. Then we who are alive and remain shall be caught up together with them in the clouds to meet the Lord in the air. And thus we shall always be with the Lord."

Isaiah 25:9 When Jesus comes the second time, the righteous will exclaim,

> "This is our God;
> We have waited for Him, and He will save us.
> This is the Lord;
> We have waited for Him;
> We will be glad and rejoice in His salvation."

Isaiah 35:10   There will be great jubilation when Jesus comes:

> The ransomed of the LORD shall return,
> And come to Zion with singing,
> With everlasting joy on their heads.
> They shall obtain joy and gladness,
> And sorrow and sighing shall flee away.

Revelation 22:7, 12, 20   Jesus' coming again is a certain event. In Revelation's last chapter, three times He says, "I am coming quickly!"

Malachi 3:2   The question is asked, "But who can endure the day of His coming? And who can stand when he appears?"

Revelation 5:9   The redeemed sing a new song, saying:

> "You are worthy to take the scroll,
> And open its seals;
> For You were slain,
> And have redeemed us to God by Your blood
> Out of every tribe and tongue and people and
>   nation,
> And have made us kings and priests to our God;
> And we shall reign on the earth."

Seven great facts regarding Jesus' second coming

1. Acts 1:9–11   It is a literal event.
2. Revelation 1:7   It is a visible event.
3. 1 Thessalonians 4:16, 17   It is an audible event.
4. Matthew 16:27   It is a glorious event.
5. Matthew 24:30, 31   It is a climactic event.
6. Isaiah 25:9   It is a joyous event.
7. Revelation 22:20   It is a certain event.

FOR FURTHER STUDY

Christ's second coming is literal

"Soon there appears in the east a small black cloud, about half the size of a man's hand. It is the cloud which surrounds the Saviour, and which seems in the distance to be shrouded in darkness. The people of God know this to be the sign of the Son of man. In solemn silence they gaze upon it as it draws nearer the earth, becoming lighter and more glorious, until it is a great white cloud, its base a glory like consuming fire, and above it the rainbow of the covenant" (*The Great Controversy*, 640, 641).

"Jesus is coming, but not as His first advent, a babe in Bethlehem; not as He rode into Jerusalem . . . ; but in the glory of the Father and with all the retinue of holy angels to escort Him on His way to earth. All heaven will be emptied of the angels, while the waiting saints will be looking for Him and gazing into heaven, as were the men of Galilee when he ascended from the Mount of Olivet" (*Early Writings*, 110).

Christ's second coming is visible

"As the living cloud comes still nearer, every eye beholds the Prince of life. No crown of thorns now mars that sacred head; but a diadem of glory rests on His holy brow. His countenance outshines the dazzling brightness of the noonday sun" (*The Great Controversy*, 641).

Christ's second coming is audible

"When Christ comes to gather to Himself those who have been faithful, the last trump will sound, and the whole earth, from the summits of the loftiest mountains to the lowest recesses of the deepest mines, will hear. The righteous dead will hear the sound of the last trump, and will come forth from their graves, to be clothed with immortality and to meet their Lord" (*The Seventh-day Adventist Bible Commentary*, vol. 7, 909).

"The voice of God is heard from heaven, declaring the day and hour of Jesus' coming, and delivering the everlasting covenant to His people. . . . And when the blessing is pronounced on those who have honored God by keeping His Sabbath holy, there is a mighty shout of victory" (*The Great Controversy*, 640).

Christ's second coming is glorious

"With anthems of celestial melody the holy angels, a vast, unnumbered throng, attend Him on His way. The firmament seems filled with radiant forms—'ten thousand times ten thousand, and thousands of thousands.' No human pen can portray the scene; no mortal mind is adequate to conceive its splendor" (*The Great Controversy*, 641).

Christ's second coming is climactic

"It is at midnight that God manifests His power for the deliverance of His people. The sun appears, shining in its strength. Signs and wonders follow in quick succession. The wicked look with terror and amazement upon the scene, while the righteous behold with solemn joy the tokens of their deliverance. Everything in nature seems turned out of its course. The streams cease to flow. Dark, heavy clouds come up and clash against each other. In the midst of the angry heavens is one clear space of indescribable glory, whence comes the voice of God like the sound of many waters, saying: 'It is done.' Revelation 16:17.

"That voice shakes the heavens and the earth. . . . The mountains shake like a reed in the wind, and ragged rocks are scattered on every side. . . . The sea is lashed into fury. There is heard the shriek of a hurricane like the voice of demons upon a mission of destruction. . . . Mountain chains are sinking. Inhabited islands disappear. . . . Great hailstones . . . are doing their work of destruction. . . . The proudest cities of the earth are laid low. . . . Prison walls are rent asunder, and God's people, who have been held in bondage for their faith, are set free" (*The Great Controversy*, 636, 637).

Christ's second coming and the wicked

"Above the terrific roar of thunder, voices, mysterious and awful, declare the doom of the wicked. The words spoken are not comprehended by all; but they are distinctly understood by the false teachers. Those who a little before were so reckless, so boastful and defiant, so exultant in their cruelty to God's commandment-keeping people, are now overwhelmed with consternation and shuddering in fear. Their wails are heard above the sound of the elements. Demons acknowledge the deity of Christ and tremble before His power, while men are supplicating for mercy and groveling in abject terror" (*The Great Controversy*, 638).

"There are those who mocked Christ in His humiliation. . . .

"Those who derided His claim to be the Son of God are speechless now. There is the haughty Herod who jeered at His royal title and bade the mocking soldiers crown Him king. There are the very men who with impious hands placed upon His form the purple robe, upon His sacred brow the thorny crown, and in His unresisting hand the mimic scepter, and bowed before Him in blasphemous mockery. The men who smote and spit upon the Prince of life now turn from His piercing gaze and seek to flee from the overpowering glory of His presence. Those who drove the nails through His hands and feet, the soldier who pierced His side, behold these marks with terror and remorse" (*The Great Controversy*, 643).

"At the coming of Christ, the wicked are blotted from the face of the whole earth—consumed with the spirit of His mouth and destroyed by the brightness of His glory" (*The Great Controversy*, 657).

Christ's second coming and the righteous

"Amid the reeling of the earth, the flash of lightning, and the roar of thunder, the voice of the Son of God calls forth the sleeping saints. He looks upon the graves of the righteous, then, raising His hands to heaven, He cries: 'Awake, awake, awake, ye that sleep in the dust, and arise!'. . .

"All come forth from their graves the same in stature as when they entered the tomb. Adam, who stands among the risen throng, is of lofty height and majestic form, in stature but little below the Son of God. He presents a marked contrast to the people of later generations; in this one respect is shown the great degeneracy of the race. But all arise with the freshness and vigor of eternal youth. . . . All blemishes and deformities are left in the grave. Restored to the tree of life in the long-lost Eden, the redeemed will 'grow up' (Malachi 4:2) to the full stature of the race in its primeval glory. The last lingering traces of the curse of sin will be removed, and Christ's faithful ones will appear in 'the beauty of the Lord our God,' in mind and soul and body reflecting the perfect image of their Lord. Oh, wonderful redemption! long talked of, long hoped for, contemplated with eager anticipation, but never fully understood.

". . . Little children are borne by holy angels to their mothers' arms. Friends long separated by death are united, nevermore to part, and with songs of gladness ascend together to the City of God" (*The Great Controversy*, 644, 645).

"The living righteous are changed 'in a moment, in the twinkling of an eye.' At the voice of God they were glorified; now they are made immortal and with the risen saints are caught up to meet their Lord in the air" (*The Great Controversy*, 645).

Christ's coming is a joyous event

"Those who would have destroyed Christ and His faithful people now witness the glory which rests upon them. In the midst of their terror they hear the voices of the saints in joyful strains exclaiming: 'Lo, this is our God; we have waited for Him, and He will save us.' Isaiah 25:9" (*The Great Controversy*, 644).

"The righteous cry with trembling: 'Who shall be able to stand?' The angels' song is hushed, and there is a period of awful silence. The voice of Jesus is heard, saying: 'My grace is sufficient for you.' The faces of the righteous are lighted up, and joy fills every heart" (*The Great Controversy*, 641).

25
Jesus Is With Us in the Millennium

John 5:28, 29	Jesus explains that "all who are in the graves will hear His voice and come forth" to one of two resurrections: "the resurrection of life" or "the resurrection of condemnation."
Revelation 1:7	Jesus "is coming with clouds, and every eye will see Him, even they who pierced Him."
1 Thessalonians 4:16	"The Lord Himself will descend from heaven with a shout, with the voice of an archangel, and with the trumpet of God. And the dead in Christ rise first."
1 Thessalonians 4:17	"Then we who are alive and remain shall be caught up together with them in the clouds to meet the Lord in the air. And thus we shall always be with the Lord."
Psalm 37:20	"The wicked shall perish" at the presence of God.
2 Thessalonians 1:7–9	Those who do not know God and obey the gospel of Jesus Christ will "be punished with everlasting destruction from the presence of the Lord and from the glory of His power."
2 Thessalonians 2:8	The lawless one (the antichrist) and all his followers will be destroyed with the brightness of Jesus' coming.
Matthew 24:31	Jesus promises that "He will send His angels with a great sound of a trumpet, and they will gather together His [people]" from all over the world.
Revelation 20:1–3	Satan, the devil, is confined to a desolate earth for a thousand years. He cannot deceive the nations anymore because no one is alive on the earth. But after one thousand years he is "released for a little while."

Jeremiah 4:23	Jeremiah refers to the desolation and total darkness in this way: "I beheld the earth, and indeed it was without form, and void; and the heavens, they had no light."
Genesis 1:2	The expression "without form, and void" is also used in Genesis 1:2. "The earth was without form, and void." This, of course, is speaking about the earth after God spoke it into existence before He created life. It was desolate. In Revelation 20:1–3, the expression is used again to describe the devil on a desolate earth, engulfed in darkness.
Revelation 20:4	During this thousand-year period, the righteous are in heaven participating with Christ in the judgment. Every question about God's justice, fairness, and love is fully answered.
Revelation 20:5	The wicked, the unsaved, do "not live again until the thousand years [are] finished."
1 Corinthians 6:2	The apostle Paul adds, "Do you not know that the saints [believers] will judge the world? And if the world will be judged by you, are you unworthy to judge the smallest matters?"
Revelation 20:7, 8	"When the thousand years have expired, Satan will be released from his prison and will go out to deceive the nations" all over the earth.
Revelation 20:9	Satan and his armies gather from all the earth and surround the camp of the saints and the Holy City. Then fire comes down from heaven and devours them.
Proverbs 11:31	The wicked receive their recompense in the earth.
Malachi 4:1	The day is coming when the wicked will be burned up. Sin and wickedness will be consumed. Satan will be finally annihilated.

Revelation 21:1, 2	There will be "a new heaven and new earth, for the first heaven and the first earth [is] passed away. . . . The holy city, the New Jerusalem, [will come] down out of heaven from God."
Revelation 21:3	God will make His home on the new earth and live with His people and be their God forever.
Revelation 19:6	A multitude of voices will be heard saying, "Alleluia! For the Lord God Omnipotent reigns!"
Revelation 7:9, 10	"A great multitude . . . of all nations, tribes, peoples, and tongues [will stand] before the throne and before the Lamb, clothed with white robes, . . . crying with a loud voice, saying, 'Salvation belongs to our God who sits on the throne, and to the Lamb!' "

FOR FURTHER STUDY

Special resurrection of those who crucified Jesus

" 'They also which pierced Him' (Revelation 1:7), those that mocked and derided Christ's dying agencies, and the most violent opposers of His truth and His people, are raised to behold Him in His glory and to see the honor placed upon the loyal and obedient" (*The Great Controversy*, 637).

The special resurrection of those who died in the three angels' messages

"The graves were opened and those who had died in the faith under the third angel's message, keeping the Sabbath, came forth from their dusty beds, glorified, to hear the covenant of peace that God was to make with those who had kept His law.

". . . And as God spoke the day and the hour of Jesus' coming and delivered the everlasting covenant to His people, He spoke one sentence, and then paused, while the words were rolling through the earth. The Israel of God stood with their eyes fixed upward, listening to the words as they came from the mouth of Jehovah and rolled through the earth like peals of loudest thunder. It was awfully solemn. At the end of every sentence the saints shouted, 'Glory! Hallelujah!' " (*Early Writings*, 285, 286).

The righteous dead

"The victory of the sleeping saints will be glorious on the morning of the resurrection. . . . The Life-giver will crown with immortality all who come forth from the grave. . . .

"There stands the risen host. The last thought was of death and its pangs. The last thoughts they had were of the grave and the tomb, but now they proclaim, 'O death, where is thy sting? O grave, where is thy victory?'. . . Here they stand and the finishing touch of immortality is put upon them and they go up to meet their Lord in the air. . . . There are the columns of angels on either side; . . . then the angelic choir strike the note of victory and the angels in the two columns take up the song and the redeemed host join as though they had been singing the song on the earth, and they have been. Oh, what music! There is not an inharmonious note. Every voice proclaims, 'Worthy is the Lamb that was slain.' He sees the travail of His soul, and is satisfied" (*Maranatha*, 300).

The wicked living

"At the coming of Christ the wicked are blotted from the face of the whole earth—consumed with the spirit of His mouth and destroyed by the brightness of His glory. Christ takes His people to the City of God, and the earth is emptied of its inhabitants" (*The Great Controversy*, 657).

The wicked dead

"At the close of the thousand years the second resurrection will take place. Then the wicked will be raised from the dead and appear before God for the execution of 'the judgment written.' Thus the revelator, after describing the resurrection of the righteous, says: 'The rest of the dead lived not again until the thousand years were finished' " (*The Great Controversy*, 661).

Jesus gathers the righteous

"With unutterable love, Jesus welcomes His faithful ones to the joy of their Lord. The Saviour's joy is in seeing, in the kingdom of glory, the souls that have been saved by His agony and humiliation. And the redeemed will be sharers in His joy, as they behold, among the blessed, those who have been won to Christ through their prayers, their labors, and their loving sacrifice. As they gather about the great white throne, gladness unspeakable will fill their hearts, when they behold those whom they have won for Christ, and see that one has gained others, and these still others, all brought into the haven of rest, there to lay their crowns at Jesus' feet and praise Him through the endless cycles of eternity" (*The Great Controversy*, 647).

Jesus welcomes the redeemed to the city of God

"As the ransomed ones are welcomed to the City of God, there rings out upon the air an exultant cry of adoration. The two Adams are about to meet. The Son of God is standing with outstretched arms to receive the father of our race—the being whom He created, who sinned against his Maker, and for whose sin the marks of the crucifixion are borne upon the Saviour's form. As Adam discerns the prints of the cruel nails, he does not fall upon the bosom of his Lord, but in humiliation casts himself at His feet, crying: 'Worthy, worthy is the Lamb that was slain!' Tenderly the Saviour lifts him up and bids him look once more upon the Eden home from which he has so long been exiled. . . .

". . . Adam is reinstated in his first dominion.

"Transported with joy, he beholds the trees that were once his delight—the very trees whose fruit he himself had gathered in the days of his innocence and joy. He sees the vines that his own hands have trained, the very flowers that he once loved to care for. His mind grasps the reality of the scene; he comprehends that this is indeed

Eden restored, more lovely now than when he was banished from it. The Saviour leads him to the tree of life and plucks the glorious fruit and bids him eat. He looks about him and beholds a multitude of his family redeemed, standing in the Paradise of God. Then he casts his glittering crown at the feet of Jesus and, falling upon His breast, embraces the Redeemer. He touches the golden harp, and the vaults of heaven echo the triumphant song: 'Worthy, worthy, worthy is the Lamb that was slain, and lives again!' The family of Adam take up the strain and cast their crowns at the Saviour's feet as they bow before Him in adoration" (*The Great Controversy*, 647, 648).

The righteous in heaven during the millennium

"During the thousand years between the first and the second resurrection the judgment of the wicked takes place. . . . John in the Revelation says, 'I saw thrones, and they sat upon them, and judgment was given unto them.'. . . Revelation 20:4. . . . It is at this time that, as foretold by Paul, 'the saints shall judge the world.' 1 Corinthians 6:2. In union with Christ they judge the wicked, comparing their acts with the statute book, the Bible, and deciding every case according to the deeds done in the body" (*The Great Controversy*, 660, 661).

Satan's final destruction

"Now Satan prepares for a last mighty struggle for the supremacy. While deprived of his power and cut off from his work of deception the prince of evil was miserable and dejected; but as the wicked dead are raised and he sees the vast multitudes upon his side, his hopes revive, and he determines not to yield the great controversy. He will marshal all the armies of the lost under his banner and through them endeavor to execute his plans. . . . He proposes to lead them against the camp of the saints and to take possession of the City of God. With fiendish exultation he points to the unnumbered millions who have been raised from the dead and declares that as their leader he is well able to overthrow the city and regain his throne and his kingdom" (*The Great Controversy*, 663).

"The wicked receive their recompense in the earth. Proverbs 11:31. They 'shall be stubble: and the day that cometh shall burn them up, saith the Lord of hosts.' Malachi 4:1. Some are destroyed as in a moment, while others suffer many days. All are punished 'according to their deeds.' The sins of the righteous having been transferred to Satan, he is made to suffer not only for his own rebellion, but for all the sins which he has caused God's people to commit. His punishment is to be far greater than that of those whom he has deceived" (*The Great Controversy*, 673).

"The fire that consumes the wicked purifies the earth. Every trace of the curse is swept away. No eternally burning hell will keep before the ransomed the fearful consequences of sin.

"One reminder alone remains: Our Redeemer will ever bear the marks of His crucifixion. Upon His wounded head, upon His side, His hands and feet, are the only traces of the cruel work that sin has wrought" (*The Great Controversy*, 674).

The redeemed in the new earth

"The redeemed raise a song of praise that echoes and re-echoes through the vaults of heaven: 'Salvation to our God which sitteth upon the throne, and unto the Lamb.' . . . And angel and seraph unite their voices in adoration. As the redeemed have beheld the power and malignity of Satan, they have seen, as never before, that no power but that of Christ could have made them conquerors. . . . Nothing is said of what they have done or suffered; but the burden of every song, the keynote of every anthem, is: Salvation to our God and unto the Lamb" (*The Great Controversy*, 665).

26
Jesus' Eternal Promise

John 14:1–3   Jesus said, "I go to prepare a place for you. And . . . I will come again and receive you to Myself; that where I am, there you may be also."

John 17:24   Jesus' desire is that His people be with Him forever in eternity. He prayed, "Father, I desire that they also whom You gave Me may be with Me where I am."

Matthew 25:34   When Jesus returns, He will give this gracious invitation to His followers. "Come, you blessed of My Father, inherit the kingdom prepared for you from the foundation of the world."

Psalm 37:29   David tells us, "The righteous shall inherit the land, and dwell in it forever."

1 Corinthians 2:9   We cannot imagine the magnificence of the glories of heaven and the earth made new. "Eye has not seen, nor ear heard, nor have entered into the heart of man the things which God has prepared for those who love Him."

1 Corinthians 15:51–54   When Jesus comes the second time, the righteous will "be changed—in a moment, in the twinkling of an eye. . . . And the dead will be raised incorruptible."

1 Corinthians 15:54   At that moment, the righteous will receive immortality, and as the apostle Paul predicted, death will be "swallowed up in victory."

Isaiah 35:4–6   We will be changed and receive new immortal bodies.

> "The eyes of the blind shall be opened,
> And the ears of the deaf shall be unstopped.
> Then the lame shall leap like a deer.
> And the tongue of the dumb sing."

Isaiah 33:24   None of the inhabitants of heaven will be sick, and the sins of those who dwell there will be forgiven.

Revelation 21:4   "God will wipe away every tear from their eyes; there shall be no more death, nor sorrow, nor crying. There shall be no more pain, for the former things have passed away."

1 Corinthians 13:12   We will recognize one another in heaven. "Now I know in part, but then I shall know just as I also am known."

John 20:16   Mary recognized Jesus after His resurrection by His voice when He called her name, "Mary."

John 20:19–21   When Jesus appeared to the disciples in the upper room, in His glorious, resurrected body, they recognized Him by His physical features.

Luke 24:16, 28–35   The disciples on the Emmaus Road did not initially recognize Jesus because "their eyes were restrained," but when He broke the bread at supper, their eyes were opened. They recognized Him by His unique mannerisms.

Philippians 3:20   The apostle Paul states an amazing truth. Today as sons and daughters of God, we are citizens of heaven, although we still live on earth. As a result, our deepest longing and most earnest desires are for Jesus to come.

Philippians 3:21   When Jesus comes, He will change our weakened, sin-polluted bodies to be like His sinless and "glorious body."

Matthew 8:11	Heaven will be a place of joy and everlasting friendship. We will have the privilege of meeting and spending time with the great men and women of faith from every generation, including such Bible characters as Abraham, Isaac, and Jacob.
Job 19:25–27	Job confidently declares, "I know that my Redeemer lives, . . . that in my flesh I shall see God."
Revelation 22:4	John adds these reassuring words, "They shall see His face."
John 20:20	The only reminder of sin in the heavenly realm is the faint scars in Jesus' hands. In His resurrected body, He showed these wound marks to His disciples.
Zechariah 13:6	The prophet records a question raised in the new earth by someone who was saved by the grace of God but never had the opportunity to hear the story of the Cross. "And one will say to him, 'What are these wounds between your arms?' Then he will answer, 'Those with which I was wounded in the house of my friends.' "
Revelation 22:5	Christ's glory is so brilliant that there will be no night in the new earth.
Revelation 21:25–27	The gates of the city will always be open and never locked because there is no need to fear foreign invaders or robbers. The new earth will be filled with people whose one purpose is to give praise to Jesus.
Isaiah 65:21, 22	In the new earth, we will build houses and live in them. We will plant vineyards and eat the abundant produce of a bountiful harvest.
Revelation 14:4	The redeemed will follow Jesus wherever He goes.
Isaiah 66:23	The Sabbath will be a time of special delight as we come to the holy city from throughout the new earth to worship. Each Sabbath, we will experience the limitless blessings of worshiping Jesus.

Revelation 21:3	Jesus will dwell with His people and be their God.
Revelation 7:9–11, 12	Revelation describes a multitude worshiping with Jesus in the new earth. The great multitude was from all nations, tribes, peoples, and tongues standing before the throne. They proclaim, "Blessing and glory and wisdom, thanksgiving and honor and power and might, be to our God forever and ever. Amen!"
Revelation 7:13, 14	"Then one of the elders answered, saying to me, 'Who are these arrayed in white robes, and where did they come from?' "And I said to him, 'Sir, you know.' "So he said to me, 'These are the ones who come out of the great tribulation, and washed their robes and made them white in the blood of the Lamb.' "
Revelation 7:15	They are the ones who stand in the presence of God because their lives are committed totally and completely to Jesus. They will worship Him continuously and live in the joy of His presence.
Revelation 21:1	God creates "a new heaven and new earth," and His people dwell with Him through the ceaseless ages of eternity.

FOR FURTHER STUDY

God's original purpose in the creation of the earth

"God's original purpose in the creation of the earth is fulfilled as it is made the eternal abode of the redeemed. 'The righteous shall inherit the land, and dwell therein forever.' Psalm 37:29" (*The Great Controversy*, 674).

"A fear of making the future inheritance seem too material has led many to spiritualize away the very truths which lead us to look upon it as our home. Christ assured His disciples that He went to prepare mansions for them in the Father's house. Those who accept the teachings of God's word will not be wholly ignorant concerning the heavenly abode. And yet, 'eye hath not seen, nor ear heard, neither have entered the heart of man, the things which God hath prepared for them that love Him.' 1 Corinthians 2:9. Human language is inadequate to describe the reward of the righteous. It will only be known to those who behold it" (*The Great Controversy*, 674, 675).

Recognizing one another in heaven

"Every saint connected in family relationship here will know each other there" (*Selected Messages*, book 3, 316).

"Our personal identity is preserved in the resurrection, though not the same particles of matter or material substance as went into the grave. The wondrous works of God are a mystery to man" (*The Seventh-day Adventist Bible Commentary*, vol. 6, 1093).

"We shall know our friends, even as the disciples knew Jesus. They may have been deformed, diseased, or disfigured, in this mortal life, and they rise in perfect health and symmetry; yet in the glorified body their identity will be perfectly preserved. . . . In the face radiant with the light shining from the face of Jesus, we shall recognize the lineaments of those we love" (*The Desire of Ages*, 804).

"The loves and sympathies which God Himself has planted in the soul shall there find truest and sweetest exercise. The pure communion with holy beings, the harmonious social life with the blessed angels and with the faithful ones of all ages who have washed their robes and made them white in the blood of the Lamb, the sacred ties that bind together 'the whole family in heaven and earth' (Ephesians 3:15)—these help constitute the happiness of the redeemed" (*The Great Controversy*, 677).

Knowing Jesus—loving Him more

"And the years of eternity, as they roll, will bring richer and still more glorious revelations of God and of Christ. As knowledge is progressive, so will love, reverence, and happiness increase. The more men learn of God, the greater will be their admiration of His character" (*The Great Controversy*, 678).

"One reminder alone remains: Our Redeemer will ever bear the marks of His crucifixion. Upon His wounded head, upon His side, His hands and feet, are the only traces of the cruel work that sin has wrought. . . . And the tokens of His humiliation are His highest honor; through the eternal ages the wounds of Calvary will show forth His praise and declare His power" (*The Great Controversy*, 674).

No night in the new earth

"In the City of God 'there shall be no night.' None will need or desire repose. There will be no weariness in doing the will of God and offering praise to His name. We shall ever feel the freshness of the morning and shall ever be far from its close. . . . The glory of God and the Lamb floods the Holy City with unfading light. The redeemed walk in the sunless glory of perpetual day" (*The Great Controversy*, 676).

Sabbath in the new earth

"And when Eden shall bloom on earth again, God's holy rest day will be honored by all beneath the sun. 'From one Sabbath to another' the inhabitants of the glorified new earth shall go up 'to worship before Me, saith the Lord.' Matthew 5:18, Isaiah 66:23" (*The Desire of Ages*, 283).

The school of the redeemed

"There, immortal minds will contemplate with never-failing delight the wonders of creative power, the mysteries of redeeming love. There will be no cruel, deceiving foe to tempt to forgetfulness of God. Every faculty will be developed, every capacity increased. The acquirement of knowledge will not weary the mind or exhaust the energies. There the grandest enterprises may be carried forward, the loftiest aspirations reached, the highest ambitions realized; and still there will arise new heights to surmount, new wonders to admire, new truths to comprehend, fresh objects to call forth the powers of mind and soul and body" (*The Great Controversy*, 677).

"All the treasures of the universe will be open to the study of God's redeemed. Unfettered by mortality, they wing their tireless flight to worlds afar—worlds that thrilled with sorrow at the spectacle of human woe and rang with songs of gladness at the tidings of a ransomed soul. With unutterable delight the children of earth enter into the joy and the wisdom of unfallen beings. They share the treasures of knowledge and understanding gained through ages upon ages in contemplation of God's handiwork" (*The Great Controversy*, 677).

"Every redeemed one will understand the ministry of angels in his own life. The angel who was his guardian from his earliest moment; the angel who watched his steps, and covered his head in the day of peril; the angel who was with him in the valley of the shadow of death, who marked his resting place, who was the first to greet him in the resurrection morning—what will it be to hold converse with him, and to learn the history of divine interposition in the individual life, of heavenly co-operation in every work for humanity!" (*Education*, 305).

Triumphant at last

"And beyond is the 'great multitude, which no man could number, of all nations, and kindreds, and people, and tongues, . . . before the throne, and before the Lamb, clothed with white robes, and palms in their hands.' Revelation 7:9. Their warfare is ended, their victory won. They have run the race and reached the prize. The palm branch in their hands is a symbol of their triumph, the white robe an emblem of the spotless righteousness of Christ which now is theirs" (*The Great Controversy*, 665).

Salvation's infinite cost

"The Lord has made every provision whereby man may have full and free salvation, and be complete in Him. . . . God has provided salvation for the world at infinite cost, even through the gift of His only-begotten Son. . . . If we are not saved, the fault will not be on the part of God, but on our part, that we have failed to cooperate with the divine agencies. Our will has not coincided with God's will" (*Selected Messages*, book 1, 375).

The earth made new

"In the final restitution, when there shall be 'a new heaven and a new earth' (Revelation 21:1), it is to be restored more gloriously adorned than at the beginning.

"Then they that have kept God's commandments shall breathe in immortal vigor beneath the tree of life; and through unending ages the inhabitants of sinless worlds shall behold, in that garden of delight, . . . a sample of what the whole earth would have become, had man but fulfilled the Creator's glorious plan" (*Patriarchs and Prophets*, 62).

"In the earth made new, the redeemed will engage in the occupations and pleasures that brought happiness to Adam and Eve in the beginning. . . .

"There every power will be developed, every capability increased. The grandest enterprises will be carried forward" (*Prophets and Kings*, 730, 731).

Bibliography

Bourdeau, D. T. "The Council at Bale, Suisse." *Advent Review and Sabbath Herald*, November 10, 1885, 12.

Nichol, Francis D., ed. *The Seventh-day Adventist Bible Commentary*. Vol. 5 of the Commentary Reference Series. Washington, DC: Review and Herald®, 1956.

White, Ellen G. *The Acts of the Apostles*. Mountain View, CA: Pacific Press®, 1911.

White, Ellen G. "Christ and the Law." *Advent Review and Herald of the Sabbath*, April 29, 1875, 138.

White, Ellen G. *Christ in His Sanctuary*. Mountain View, CA: Pacific Press®, 1969.

White, Ellen G. "Christ Our Only Hope." *Signs of the Times*, August 2, 1905, 9, 10.

White, Ellen G. *Christian Education*. Battle Creek, MI: International Tract Society, 1893.

White, Ellen G. *Colporteur Ministry*. Mountain View, CA: Pacific Press®, 1953.

White, Ellen G. *Counsels for the Church*. Mountain View, CA: Pacific Press®, 1957.

White, Ellen G. *Counsels on Diet and Foods*. Washington, DC: Review and Herald®, 1938.

White, Ellen G. "The Day of the Lord Is Near, and Hasteth Greatly." *Advent Review and Sabbath Herald*, November 24, 1904, 16, 17.

White, Ellen G. *The Desire of Ages*. Oakland, CA: Pacific Press®, 1898.

White, Ellen G. *Early Writings*. Battle Creek, MI: Review and Herald®, 1882.

White, Ellen G. *Education*. Oakland, CA: Pacific Press®, 1903.

White, Ellen G. "Ellen G. White Comments—1 Corinthians." In *The Seventh-day Adventist Bible Commentary*. Vol. 6 of the Commentary Reference Series, edited by Francis D. Nichol. Washington, DC: Review and Herald®, 1957.

White, Ellen G. "Ellen G. White Comments—1 Thessalonians." In *The Seventh-day Adventist Bible Commentary*. Vol. 7 of the Commentary Reference Series, edited by Francis D. Nichol. Washington, DC: Review and Herald®, 1957.

White, Ellen G. Ellen G. White to Brethren of the General Conference. Melbourne, Australia. December 19, 1892. Letter 32, 1892.

White, Ellen G. Ellen G. White to Brother and Sister Lacey. Sunnyside, Cooranbong, New South Wales, Australia. March 23, 1897. Letter 89c, 1897.

White, Ellen G. *Evangelism*. Washington, DC: Review and Herald®, 1946.

White, Ellen G. "The Government of God." *Advent Review and Sabbath Herald*, March 9, 1886, 1, 2.

White, Ellen G. *The Great Controversy Between Christ and Satan*. Mountain View, CA: Pacific Press®, 1911.

White, Ellen G. "The Great Need of the Holy Spirit." *Advent Review and Sabbath Herald*, July 23, 1895, 1, 2.

White, Ellen G. *Last Day Events*. Boise, ID: Pacific Press®, 1992.

White, Ellen G. *Maranatha: The Lord Is Coming*. Washington, DC: Review and Herald®, 1976.

White, Ellen G. "Marvelous Outpouring of Spiritual Power." *Signs of the Times*, February 17, 1914, 3.

White, Ellen G. *The Ministry of Healing*. Mountain View, CA: Pacific Press®, 1905.

White, Ellen G. *Patriarchs and Prophets*. Battle Creek, MI: Review and Herald®, 1890.

White, Ellen G. *Prophets and Kings*. Mountain View, CA: Pacific Press®, 1917.

White, Ellen G. "Recount God's Dealings." *Advent Review and Sabbath Herald*, March 19, 1895, 1, 2.

White, Ellen G. *Reflecting Christ*. Hagerstown, MD: Review and Herald®, 1985.

White, Ellen G. *Selected Messages*, book 1. Washington, DC: Review and Herald®, 1958.

White, Ellen G. *Selected Messages*, book 3. Washington, DC: Review and Herald®, 1980.

White, Ellen G. *Steps to Christ*. Oakland, CA: Pacific Press®, 1892.

White, Ellen G. *The Story of Redemption*. Washington, DC: Review and Herald®, 1947.

White, Ellen G. *Testimonies for the Church*. 9 vols. Mountain View, CA: Pacific Press®, 1948.

White, Ellen G. *Thoughts From the Mount of Blessing*. Oakland, CA: Pacific Press®, 1896.

White, Ellen G. "What Was Secured by the Death of Christ." *Signs of the Times*, December 30, 1889, 1, 2.

White, Ellen G. "The Word Made Flesh." *Signs of the Times*, May 3, 1899, 1, 2.